FROM DEBUTANTE
TO
DOUBLEWIDE

Kathy
Grizzard
Schmook

 Peachtree Publishers, Ltd.

Published by
PEACHTREE PUBLISHERS, LTD.
494 Armour Circle, N.E.
Atlanta, Georgia 30324

Manufactured in the United States of America

10 9 8 7 6 5 4 3 2

Library of Congress Catalog Card Number 87-80975

ISBN 0-934601-27-5

For Curly,
the kindest person I've ever known.

FROM DEBUTANTE
TO
DOUBLEWIDE

CHAPTER I

Bright Lights, Big City

IT STARTED IN my exercise studio the day my gravity boots lost their pull. I landed on my head and a thin piece of AstroTurf that covered the concrete floor. Not a great way to start a Monday, but it did scramble my brain enough to force a painful realization . . . my life wasn't fun anymore, and I needed to change it.

Being a divorced mother of two in a city of millions had me frazzled. The highlight of my day was going home after work to my intown condominium and hearing from my children—Lisa, twelve, and Bruce, ten — the tales of rape and robbery in our complex. The kids were always disappointed that we were never the victims because then we could have been on the six o'clock news along with our neighbors. I figured our chance would come soon enough.

I also had to face the fact that some of the things I held most precious—things that helped me cope with Atlanta—were slipping away from me. I wept the day Juanda told me she was retiring from her tray of sculptured nails. She had met the man of her dreams at Club Med, and they were going to be married and move to Barrow, Alaska, to open a tanning salon. How could I ever touch my computer again without the fourteen-carat gold fingernail only Juanda could apply to my little finger?

Then there was Dr. Pullit, my aging but discreet cosmetic surgeon. How sad I was to hear of the malpractice suit that forced him out of business. I thought his idea of the party breasts was cute. He inserted a balloon into the breast along with a small pump so that you could do your errands and attend meetings without being distractingly voluptuous. Then, when the sun went down and the occasion called for "more," the wearer simply pumped herself up and, bingo, centerfold material! Unfortunately, one of his patients became rather amorous on a flight from Atlanta to Los Angeles and went into the lavatory to pump up. Somehow the drinks or the pressure in the cabin got the best of her, and the rest was horrifying. Yes, they exploded somewhere over Arizona. Dr. Pullit, I understand, settled out of court to avoid an embarrassing courtroom slide show.

I loved my job in the travel industry; it was never a problem. However, trying to park near my office was a constant challenge. If they had never installed the new ticket machine with the electronic arm, things would have been fine. I tried to be like the other people who drove in, slid their card in the slot and waited for the automated arm to lift before they drove through. But it never worked for me. I tried in vain every day for two weeks to make that arm lift by shoving in my card and . . . nothing. The disgusted attendant always had to come over and jam his master card in to open the arm for me.

People behind me would blow their horns at me and yell insults like "Why don't you stick it in your . . ." Finally, on a hot August morning, I snapped. I drove through the arm. The attendant caught up to me as I wheeled into a convenient space. His behavior did not reflect the fact that I was paying him more than Juanda and Dr. Pullit combined.

My children, both in a private school, were incensed that we were not in Kitzbühel skiing over Christmas like everybody else, and they were not buying my story that a trip to Grandpapa's farm in Suches, Georgia, was just as exciting as the Virgin Islands over spring break or picking up a new Mercedes in Stuttgart during summer vacation. Their tuition ran neck and neck with the cost of refurbishing the Statue of Liberty, and I had my young son at the psychologist once a week trying to figure out why he had the jitters in class and continued to throw small, homegrown patio tomatoes at his teacher when her back was turned. I was upset but not surprised when I got one of those "We think little Bruce would be happier in another learning situation" letters, which in plain English means "That brat is outa' here."

For me, romance was a mere fantasy. By the time I was finished with carpool lines, the shrink (mine as well as Bruce's), the dentist, my Junior League meetings, baseball practice, dancing lessons (Lisa's, not Bruce's), and a full day of work, who could date? I couldn't carry on a conversation with Big Bird after a day of that.

Finally, I wised up and discovered the most wonderful thing since sandalfoot pantyhose—a housekeeper. She did all the mundane, day-to-day chores, and all I had to do was work twelve hours a day, six days a week, to pay her. Still, it made sense to me until my accountant asked me if I understood that my housekeeper was in the 40 percent tax bracket, and I was headed for food stamps. And then . . . she was gone. She decided that she would be happier working in her Uncle Vladpatch's Yak Takey Outey back in her native Afghanistan. After having to pay twenty-five hundred dollars for an immigration lawyer to get Shludna back to her homeland, I was broke, bumfuzzled, and bored! I wasn't living, I was just putting in time, and I began to wonder, "Is life always going to be like this?"

Then one day as I sat giving myself a pedicure and opening the mail at my office desk, a particularly intriguing travel brochure fell into my lap. It advertised a hidden guest ranch in the Rocky Mountains of Montana near Yellowstone Park. The pictures of the sagebrush and sunsets, the horses and a cloud-shrouded swimming hole, the streams and log cabins captivated me. I called my accountant for advice on withdrawing money from my meager savings account, and after he said it would be financial suicide, I made reservations for Lisa, Bruce, and me to head west for three weeks that coming summer.

The ranch was better than I imagined. Trips down the Yellowstone River and through the park were unforgettable. There were horseback trips into the mountains, square dances, sumptuous meals cooked outside over a campfire, and, above all, there were friendly, unpretentious people who had never given a second thought to the upward mobility that seemed to dominate Atlanta's caste system. Why, after the first two days, I was able to put away my totebag of cosmetics, including the sixty-color eyeshadow palette I got for only twenty dollars when I purchased fifty dollars of special Estee Lauder skin-care treatments, and my Oil of Olay became nothing more than a faint memory. No one seemed to notice that I had the eyes of a chicken without my makeup, and they didn't seem to care that I had thrown caution to the wind and wore only clear polish on my unwrapped, unsculptured nails.

But, as luck would have it, an unforeseen element entered the picture that August as I frolicked among the flora and fauna of the little idyllic hideaway: I met a man. Just what I needed . . . something else to complicate my already exasperating life. I had a collection of alimony and child support checks that rivaled Zsa Zsa Gabor's, and the last thing I needed was to run into yet another hormonal hazard.

His name was Fred, and he managed the little ranch. He had been employed by IBM years earlier, then had continued with a series of unrewarding desk jobs. After his marriage dissolved, he headed to the hills, and that is where he had been for the last few years. Armed with this information, supplied by my trusty sidekicks, Bruce and Lisa, I figured a brief dalliance would be harmless in the middle of nowhere. And, too, he was different from other men I had known. No smooth talk, no Dun and Bradstreet report, and no hair. But there was something about the way the skin around his eyes crinkled when he smiled, due to many years of exposure to the wind and sun. And when his rough, calloused hand held mine, I felt strangely vulnerable yet secure at the same time.

He was a man of few words, but when he spoke the conversation didn't center around him and what he had done or where he had been. He was genuinely interested in my children and me. No one had asked me so much about them since the doctors in the emergency room when I had to take Bruce in for stitches after Lisa closed him up in his Swing-o-Matic when he was only three months old and cracked his head open. Fred was curious about where I came from and how I had ended up in Montana, and as I unfolded my rather lurid past for him, I began to realize I had more skeletons in my closet than the Harvard Medical School. He seemed understanding, and as the days went on, I learned he was a man who said what he meant and meant what he said. He said he liked me and would keep in touch. Somehow I knew he would.

Lisa and Bruce were doing their best to aid and abet the relationship. Bruce was busy telling Fred, "Mom is a great cook! She can cook everything from a Manwich sandwich to Spaghettios!" And Lisa, the perpetual romantic, tried to allay any fears that I might want more children by telling Fred, "Don't worry, she's been fixed."

I left the ranch with my emotions intact, although I was more relaxed, less cynical, a bit wistful. I had seen a dimension of life I had never known before, and somehow it seemed that life in the land of Indian lore, undeveloped frontier, and men that thought Calvin Klein was a Nazi hunter was indeed slower and had more quality to it.

"Oh, well," I thought, as my plane taxied down the runway and Bruce and Lisa began fighting in the seats next to me, "just another bunch of pictures I can develop and stick in my album next to the ones of that exciting trip we took last summer to see *Unto These Hills* at the Cherokee Indian reservation." But the memory of the mountains and the pungent smell of the forests haunted me after my return to the traffic, crime, and rampant lust for materialism I was surrounded by. I was living one life and longing for another.

True to his word, Fred did keep in touch. We had phone bills some months that were nearly as high as the children's tuition and my parking bill together. After a while it was simply cheaper for me to visit.

On one of those trips, in a romantic bar in Twodot, Montana, Fred asked me to marry him. I told him to give me a few days and I would let him know. It was hard to think with so much Hank Williams, Jr., blaring in the background. The next day I went for a long, soul-searching walk. As I wandered alone late into the afternoon, I watched a gold and pink glow settle on the top of some snow-capped mountains in the distance, and a light snow began to fall. I felt the tears of frustration begin because I had the feeling I would never be back. I felt a lot like Catherine did when she had Heathcliff lug her over to the windows to catch a final glimpse of the moors before she croaked.

Finally, confident I had made a decision my mother would approve, I returned to Fred's cozy little log cabin and recited every cornball rejection I could think of . . . "I will always love you, but . . ."; "It's not you, it's me"; "If I didn't have the kids . . .," and my big finish "This is just another one of life's injustices" (I knew I was really scraping the bottom there). The beast replied "You and your children will always have a home here with me if you want it." And he took me to the airport.

I moped around for the next few weeks trying to convince myself I had made the right decision, but my mind kept going back to the kind, baldheaded man who had traded his cowboy hat in on the

Atlanta Falcons cap I had taken him. And his eyes. I kept seeing them with the crinkles around them, and I remembered that they looked awfully wet when he said good-bye at the gate.

Two weeks after my arrival home, the phone rang on my desk at work, and I was surprised to hear it was Bruce's shrink, Dr. Dorfmeicher. He said he was getting ready to close his practice and leave town, and he was just calling some of his best customers to say good-bye. I was stunned and asked where he was going. He said that he was moving near Villa Rica, Georgia, to take over his uncle's Roto-Rooter business. He simply could not listen to one more neurotic crackpot describe a list of ailments. He had, it seemed, crossed over that dangerous line. One day he snapped during a session and told his patient to "put up or shut up." The pressure had simply gotten to him, and he wanted to leave while he was young enough to start a new career away from the city. He wanted to slow the pace of his life down. I hung up and pondered what Dr. Dorfmeicher had said. If he thought he was a mess at twenty-eight, at thirty-eight I must be a raving lunatic!

That night I picked up the kids from my mother's, fixed dinner, and put everyone to bed early, including myself. I sat in bed and looked through the mail, which was a grave error, or so I thought. In my hand was Dr. Dorfmeicher's final bill, an overdue notice on the tuition from the school that had just booted Bruce, my Junior League dues invoice, which had doubled, a request for a contribution to the "Help Keep Atlanta's Bathhouses Open Cause," and an invitation to a fundraiser for one of my ex-husbands who was running for governor. That did it.

I snatched up my telephone and started punching buttons as fast as I could, only to get a busy signal on the other end. I was frantic; I punched again. Finally, I punched with a ferocity Ma Bell had never known . . . and the phone at the other end rang. "Fred!" I screamed hysterically. "Take me, I'm yours—forever!" The voice on the other end said quietly, "Just a moment, and I'll get my son." I was embarrassed but undaunted. Then I heard him. "Fred, is that you?" I cried.

"Yep, but what's wrong?" he asked, obviously concerned.

"Remember all that stupid stuff I told you week before last? Well, forget it. I didn't mean it. I changed my mind. I love you, and I want us to be a family."

"You're sure you're ready to trade in a Saturday night of fancy dinners and discos for some elk hunting?" he asked gently.

"I can't wait!" I said, undeterred, hoping I would learn the difference in an elk, a deer, and a moose.

"And you'll help old Bruce and me fry up those trout we're gonna reel in, huh?"

"Why, I love to fish," I lied, thinking back on man's most boring sport, which even TV can't make look good on *The Great American Sportsman.*

"And you won't mind getting up in the middle of the night to throw some more wood in the stove during a winter storm?" he asked.

"Of course not—I love snow!" At least I did the time I skied on it in the sporting goods store when I bought my new ski pants, I thought.

"Well, I'd be mighty proud if you and your little dudes would move out here with an old-timing man like me, and I promise I'll do my damnedest to make you the three happiest folks west of the Mississippi."

We decided he'd come down and get me in a month, so the next few weeks were a whirlwind, with the highlight being the night I announced to my family that I was leaving for the wilds of Montana. My mother looked at me as if I'd inhaled an overabundance of Sweet 'N Low before she swooned, my father asked me if I realized that even Ward Bond's Wagon Train wouldn't cross Montana in the winter, and my darling but aged grandmother thought it was sweet that I was going to marry a football star named after a state. The rest of my friends and family asked only that this be my last marriage because they couldn't afford any more wedding presents. I assured them that this was the last name change of my career. The IRS was going to be thrilled.

What adventures awaited me?

Would Lisa, who was engulfed in puberty, and Bruce, a borderline juvenile delinquent and latent pyromaniac, be as happy feeding their horses as they were feeding themselves at the Piedmont Driving Club?

Would the bugle of an elk have the same elec-trifying effect as the whirr of the escalator going up to the designer salon at Neiman-Marcus?

Could a trained Junior League volunteer find ful-fillment in attempting to change Yellowstone National Park into a petting zoo?

The answers to these gut-wrenching questions and many more are found in the following pages. For others who may be ready to trade their Perrier for ditch and a make-up brush for sagebrush, I offer this guidebook, a how-to for the modern-day pioneer with panache.

CHAPTER II

Wagons Ho

IT WAS HARD to shed a tear or feel much remorse as our caravan pulled out of my condominium in Atlanta to begin the trip west. I was a bundle of nerves as Fred followed my car down busy city streets and in and out of traffic. He was driving the world's largest Hertz rental truck, the one once used to move the Marcos family from Manila to their temporary home in Hawaii, and, in addition, he was pulling a large trailer to house the cumulative wedding gifts I had acquired throughout the years but had never bothered to unpack. Somehow, the minute I unpacked a wedding gift and really got the hang of using it, especially if it was monogrammed, a malevolent spell was cast upon the marriage; therefore, I stopped opening presents, but I decided to take them west along with the rest of my earthly belongings.

Fred had not recently driven in a city with a population over five thousand; most of the pedestrians he knew had been horses and cows. Suddenly, he was wheeling around a city of two million people. I guess we were lucky that he only sideswiped one bus and a Domino's Pizza delivery car and scraped off just a little bit on the underside of the parking deck at the Varsity, where I had to stop for one last chili dog with onion rings and a pc/ic (plain chocolate with ice cream). That was the only time I shed a tear, and I made Fred promise that upon my death he would hold curbside services for me there.

Once we were on the interstate, I relaxed a bit. We decided the children would ride with me for a while, then Fred. Unfortunately, Fred's rental truck had no air conditioning, no radio, and went over fifty miles an hour only when it was going downhill. The children rode with me most of the time.

One of the most abhorrent things that can happen to a parent is to be stuck in a car with children for any period of time, especially if they're excited. Lisa, who could talk the ears off a chicken, was chattering nonstop about how she was going to decorate her new room and that she felt a slumber party was in order immediately upon arrival so that she could meet new friends. Bruce played cowboy and Indian behind the back seat, using an empty BB gun and making all the appropriate sound effects.

As we drove throughout the day and the kids became restless, I suggested they play car bingo or the license plate game that I had purchased before we left. Then I went through a light lecture on the geography of places we were passing, like Chattanooga, Nashville, and Paducah, Kentucky. That met with a lot of negative reaction. Then Lisa said, "Mom, that is so boring. Why don't you talk about sex?"

"What?" I bellowed, hoping I had misunderstood my pre-adolescent daughter.

"Yeah, you could tell Bruce all that stuff you told me that time . . . he doesn't know anything at all, I'll bet."

"I do too, creepface. I know more than you do!" Bruce yelled, and he made an internationally recognized obscene gesture.

"Hey, cut that out! Bruce," I said, knowing I was taking my life in my hands, "do you think you are mature enough to discuss sex without acting silly or making jokes about it?"

"Sure, and besides, I've seen that Dr. Ruth lady on TV . . . she tells lots of big sex words. And you know what else I've seen?"

I shuddered and said, "No."

"Whenever I go to Grandpapa's farm, he always has that station on his satellite with naked people on it, and guess what, one time I saw two men kissing, and . . ."

"*Bruce!* Stop that, right now. What in the world is your grandfather doing while you're looking at that trash?"

"Oh, he's watching too."

Wait till the next time I speak to my father, I thought. "Well, Bruce that is not what sex is about."

"See, I told you you didn't know anything," Lisa interjected. "What's a prophylactic, smarty?"

"Lisa!" I tried to interrupt.

"I think it's that jelly stuff you rub on so you don't have a baby," Bruce answered pensively.

I decided to use very accurate and technical terms and said, "Bruce, that's not quite right. Another word for it is a condom, and . . ."

"Oh, you mean a rubber!" he answered. "I know all about those. We put one on a corn dog in the cafeteria one time at school," he announced proudly, and I began to understand why it was suggested that he continue his education at another learning institution.

"Do you want to learn anything, or are you just going to act silly? I am not going to discuss the beauty and intimacy of the sexual experience if you are going to talk dirty," I warned.

"I already know all that junk, Mom," Bruce said. "Tell some good stuff."

I began with the Adam and Eve story and tried to update to modern times by conveying the miracle of their own births. I used biological terms, and at one point Lisa said, "Gross, Mom, did you ever do that?"

"Well, of course, honey, how do you think you got here?"

"I don't know . . . I never thought about you, though. And you did it with Dad? Ugh, gross me out."

I silently reproached myself for ever beginning the discussion. As I tried to end it, Bruce said, "There's only one thing I want to know."

"What's that, honey?" I asked.

"Can kids watch?"

"Bruce! Did you not listen to one thing I said? I told you that sex is the strongest way of saying 'I love you' between a husband and a wife, a very private thing, so obviously no one else watches!"

Luckily, a Holiday Inn appeared on the horizon, and I pulled off into the parking lot at about fifty miles an hour in a rather addled state. Fred followed us and climbed out of the steaming cab of his truck.

"What did you pull in here for?" he asked. "I told you we have to stay at truck stops because that outfit I'm driving won't fit in a conventional motel parking lot."

"Sorry," I said, "but my nerves couldn't take it any longer. Masters and Johnson in the back seat had me so confused you're lucky I made it this far."

"Well, you did great. I can't believe you drove all this way in one day, honey. I'm real proud of you."

"Time does fly when you're having sex, uh, fun," I said, and Fred looked at me strangely. "Besides, Freddy, my sweet, I don't want to spend the first night of our honeymoon in a truck stop. Couldn't we stay here tonight?"

"All right, but I'll have to find a parking lot to park in. You go get us all checked in and I'll meet you in the lobby."

The check-in process was predictably traumatic.

"We want our own room, Mom," Lisa announced as I signed the register.

No one on the face of the earth wanted Lisa and Bruce to have their own room more than I did. However, I was still paying my Visa bill from the only time I ever left them in a hotel room alone.

"No, you can't stay in your own room. You're too young. Remember what happened in Savannah?" I said firmly.

The past spring I had stopped to spend the night in Savannah on the way to Florida. I decided to go for a jog before dinner, so I left the children in the room innocently playing Monopoly. I told them I would be gone for an hour and made them promise not to leave the room. When I returned, I knocked on the door. No answer. I knocked again, and a voice said, "Enter, your protuberance," as Bruce slowly opened the door.

I gasped at the sight of the banquet-sized table set up in the small double room.

"What's going on?" I asked, totally perplexed.

"We ordered room service, Mom. Look, Lisa even ordered you some champagne," Bruce said.

I sat down heavily on the bed and put my face in my hands, hoping the table was a mirage . . . it didn't go away. As I surveyed the prime rib, steak, hamburger, and fried chicken dinner, I glanced at the television set, which was tuned in to some station with a lot of naked people walking around in space helmets.

"What in heaven's name is on that television?" I asked in a barely audible voice, feeling as though I were going to faint.

Lisa, who was glued to the set and gnawing on a chicken drumstick, said, "*Flesh Gordon* . . . Bruce pushed the buttons for the adult movie and this came on. It's really cool. We thought you'd like it since you're an adult. Aren't you glad we didn't make you look at some Walt Disney movie?"

"Yeah," Bruce added. "But what does 'your protuberance' mean? They keep saying that in the movie."

I firmly pressed the "off" button and picked up the seventy-five-dollar room-service bill, which I later tried to negotiate with the front desk, but to no avail. The memory of it all hadn't faded, so not even my honeymoon was reason enough to put the kids in a room alone. However, I forgot to clear my plan with the groom.

Fred met us out in front of the motel and said, "I had to park way down the street there in a Kroger parking lot, but I think it'll be safe." He winked at me and squeezed my hand and said, "Let's go to our room, wash up a bit, maybe have a beer, then we'll have some supper. How does that sound, kids? Maybe you guys would like to hop in that swimming pool I saw around back."

"We don't want to," Lisa said. "We'll just go with y'all."

"Well, Mom and I will get you settled in your room and . . ."

"We're in your room!" Bruce announced. "Mom wouldn't let us have our own. That's not fair, is it, Fred?"

"What?" Fred howled.

"Sweetie pie, I just didn't feel like I could trust a ten-year-old and a twelve-year-old in a room alone." I leaned over and whispered in his ear, "Besides, they'll be asleep early, they're tired."

Fred gave me a weak smile and said, "Let's just go have dinner now, in that case, so we can turn in early . . . we've got a long day tomorrow." We left for a subdued meal at Pizza Hut.

When we returned, Bruce jumped on one of the quilted blue-and-green floral bedspreads and said, "Can I have this bed by the bathroom?"

Fred said, "Sure," as he sat down wearily on the other bed. I turned on the television, kissed the kids good-night, then changed into my "trousseau" nightie in the bathroom. I got into bed with Fred and nestled my head on his shoulder.

"Why do you still have your clothes on?" I whispered.

"Because I've never been around a young girl before, and she is still awake. She keeps staring at me."

We watched television for a while and took turns glancing at the kids, who never took their eyes off us.

"Hi, Mom," Lisa would say when I looked at her.

"Hi, Lisa," I'd say.

At about one A.M. Lisa piped up with, "I see that, Mom."

"See what?" I asked.

"Your covers are moving all around."

"Do you mind if we breathe?" Fred asked in growing frustration, still completely clothed.

Lisa returned to her guard position, leaning on one elbow and staring at us. I silently kicked myself for ever mentioning the word *sex* in the car.

Fred finally snapped. "O.K.! That's enough . . . I've had it. Lisa, come get in bed with your mother. Bruce, you're gonna sleep with me. I'll be right back, I'm gonna take a shower."

"Can I take one, too?" Bruce asked.

"No, you won't want to . . . this one is going to be freezing cold." He stomped into the bathroom and slammed the door.

These sleeping arrangements continued for four nights. Fred and I were reduced to behaving like illicit adolescent lovers as we stole passionate kisses, sheltered by the concrete blocks that separate the men's and women's restrooms at truck stops. Once Fred bought the kids twenty-five dollars worth of firecrackers and allowed them to shoot them off in a convenience store parking lot only so we could sneak behind the ice machine for a quick body press, nothing more. It didn't help as we drove through hundreds of miles of cornfields and pastures filled with cattle. Bruce would nudge Lisa, and together they would smirk, one of them chiming in with, "Hey, Mom, what are those cows doing?" I dared not look. Each night was the same, cold shower for Fred, and each morning, another cold shower for Fred. On the last morning Lisa said, "Mom, Fred must be an Eskimo. He likes lots of cold water."

I answered, "No, he's no Eskimo, but he's beginning to think he's married one, I'm afraid." On the fifth day of travel, as we approached our new home in Montana, I wondered if we had broken the Guinness record on taking the longest amount of time in history to consummate a marriage. I figured this must be a form of punishment for having more than one official honeymoon. I think I read that you shouldn't in Proverbs.

Has Anyone Here Seen My Doublewide?

To drive twenty-five hundred miles across the country and suddenly realize you don't exactly know where you're going is a very strange sensation. As we entered the valley that was to become our home, I motioned to Fred to pass us since I didn't know how to get to the house . . . in fact I had never seen anything more than a snapshot of it. Moving into a house sight unseen is quite unusual for a woman who has spent years consulting a decorator about which color of Scott towels to put in her perfectly coordinated kitchen and who traveled to Greece to handpick a needlepoint rug crafted by artisans on the island of Hydra. However, there was that irresistible mesmerizing influence from the mountains. As we drove through them, the kids and I remarked to each other that they looked like the phony front of a movie set . . . almost as if they had been painted against the sky.

Fred turned off the highway, drove about a mile, then turned down a dirt road, lined with wooden fences on either side. He pulled the enormous truck and the tag-along trailer into a little grove of delicate trees with white bark. I later learned these trees are aspens. He climbed out of the truck and scratched his head. I had learned in five days of non-conjugal bliss that a head scratch meant problems.

"I'll be damned," Fred said, frowning.

"What's the matter, honey?" I asked as the kids and I walked over to him. "Where are we?"

"Well, this is home, but the house isn't here yet," he said. I thought this statement was a little idiotic. "But that little log building over there, that's the finest outhouse in Montana."

"I can see there is no house. Do people live in their outhouses? What's going on?" I asked, getting concerned.

"I didn't want to worry you, but I bought that house I sent you the picture of, and I paid to have it moved to this beautiful piece of property. I guess those damn guys didn't get it here on time . . . I swear if they're drunk again, I'll kill 'em!"

My lips barely parted as I said, "Drunk? Moving a house . . . my house? The house I drove across the country to move into?"

"Oh, baby, don't worry. I told the folks at the saloon not to serve Cleve and Steve anything on moving day."

"Who are Steve and Cleve?" I asked.

"They're the guys I paid to move the house. They do it all the time, but they have been known to take a drink now and then."

At that moment a very attractive lady in jeans and a cowboy hat rode up on a big buckskin horse.

"Hi," she said with a smile. "This must be your new family, Fred . . . glad to see you guys made it."

I had been rendered speechless by the Case of the Drunken House Delivery and could only nod.

"Sarah, have you seen the house anywhere?" Fred asked.

She replied, very nonchalantly, "Yeah, Steve and Cleve had some trouble with their truck . . . starter went out. So they had to unload the house at the top of the road back there and kick the truck off. They should be loadin' the house back up anytime now. They have to 'cause the sheriff said he was gonna ticket them for blockin' the road. The house is set right in the middle of it." I felt myself begin to get lightheaded, and then I heard, "In fact, Jerry Pittley just had to move 'bout a dozen head of cattle through it . . . went right in the front door, through the living room, and out the back door in the kitchen."

The next sound was a soft thud as I landed at Fred's feet in a dead faint.

"Kathy, honey, come on now, it'll be all right," he gently urged as he rubbed my forehead with a calico handkerchief. "I can fix or rebuild anything that is damaged in the move. Now, come on, get up."

Bruce came running up the dirt path with two other boys about his own age, and he yelled, "Mom, this is Ralph and Frankie . . . can I get my hair cut like theirs?" The boys had a couple of authentic Mohawks, and Bruce was ready to make an Indian transformation on the spot.

"Your ma's not feelin' too good right now," Sarah said. "If she says it's OK later, I'll give you one . . . I did my boys."

Suddenly Lisa yelled and pointed up the road, "Look, I bet that's our house!"

"Yep, sure is," Fred said as he helped me to my feet.

Very slowly a large truck began to turn the corner at the top of the hill. As it made the turn, it took a good many power lines with it.

"Uh-oh," Sarah said, "I better go call the power company. I can already tell we won't have any power around here for a while."

I was still speechless and merely stared as the truck with a two-story house behind it made its way down the hill toward us. The closer it got, the more relieved I felt. It was much more appealing than the picture Fred had sent me. It was a charming little yellow Victorian farmhouse with a white gingerbread front porch. It didn't seem to be too damaged by the move, even though it did have a few utility wires draped across it. The front door was also missing. The truck pulled into the driveway, a barrage of beer cans flying out of both windows.

"How do you like it?" Fred asked with pride in his voice.

I was able to find my own voice somewhere and said, "Well, it's . . . it's . . . not like any other house I've ever had."

"Great!" Fred beamed. "That's what I hoped. I'll fix this little house up to where it'll sparkle for you! There's just one thing, though. We're gonna have to use the outhouse till I get the plumbing hooked up right."

I grimaced and managed a "Fine."

Steve and Cleve alighted from the truck and asked Fred exactly where the house was supposed to sit. Fred showed them, and they said that since the positioning was going to take some tricky maneuvers, they'd come back first thing in the morning to do the actual unloading.

"But, Fred," I managed, "where will we spend the night?"

"Right here in that doublewide," Sarah said, and she gestured to a large mobile home in a pasture about a quarter of a mile away. "It's ours, and we rent it out. No one is in it right now . . . you're welcome to spend the night, and we'll get you all unloaded tomorrow."

"I couldn't impose on you like that," I started.

"Just leave everything where you've got it, come on over to my house for supper, then have a good night's sleep."

Before I could argue, Steve and Cleve said they were leaving and would be back at eight the next morning. "Need a ride home?" Fred asked.

"Nope," Cleve answered. "Gonna walk down to the saloon . . . catch a ride from there."

"Come on, you guys, I know you're exhausted," Sarah said. "Let's go to my house and have supper, and, Kathy, you can meet my husband, Ken."

Fred took my hand, and he and I followed Sarah while she rode back to her house with all the kids circling.

"I'm too tired to eat, Fred," I said. "I just want to go to bed."

We arrived at Sarah's, and Fred shook hands with her husband, Ken. They had been friends for a long time, and I noticed they were speaking softly to each other away from the rest of us. Then I heard Ken say to all four children, "How'd you kids like to sleep in the hayloft of our new barn?"

"Wow, can we, Mom? They got a baby horse out there!" Lisa and Bruce exclaimed in unison.

Frankly, I didn't care if they slept on top of the barn's weather vane. All I knew was I had to find a bed fast.

"Sure you can," Fred answered for me. "We'll see you early in the morning 'cause we'll need you to help get your rooms straight."

Since Sarah had no power, thanks to Steve and Cleve, we had a wonderful cold supper of vegetables from Sarah's garden, after which Fred led me through a field to our shelter for the night.

"You know, Kathy," Fred said as he opened the front door, "this may look like just a doublewide to you, but it looks like heaven to me." He slammed the door and locked it.

At exactly seven-thirty the next morning, four children stood out in front of our mobile love nest. "Mom, wake up. Sarah said it was time for breakfast . . . those men are gonna be back to unpack our house."

I had hoped that perhaps the situation with the house had been part of a dream, but as I dressed and walked up to Sarah's with Fred, I was able to look down through several pastures and see our home still sitting behind the cab of a truck. Luckily, the power had been restored, and Sarah and Ken fixed a delicious breakfast of raspberry pancakes. Steve and Cleve arrived around eight o'clock and began the task of unloading the house. I literally couldn't watch. They took until four o'clock that afternoon to get the house on the foundation Fred had prepared.

When they left, I stood and stared at the battered building. I could not imagine how we'd ever unpack all our furniture and get settled in a new house that was showing lots of mileage. Then I heard a thundering of engines. Up the dirt lane came a parade of pickup trucks, tractors, and horses with riders. People I had never laid eyes on before appeared from nowhere, all asking Fred where to begin unloading. Fred opened the backs of our Hertz trailer and truck, pointed to the house, and, before I knew it, furniture, boxes, and food were being unloaded and moved in.

"Fred, where did all these people come from?" I asked in shock.

"Well, I had Ken go down to the saloon and empty it out . . . never find better help anywhere."

"But there are ladies and kids and . . . how will I ever thank them?"

"No need. They'll be able to use help one day, too. Besides, I bought two cases of beer to thank the guys. It's amazing how much work a little beer can get out of people."

I tried to imagine the same scene taking place in the city. The idea was ludicrous. Nothing like that happened unless people were paid by the hour. I stood and watched helplessly. Everyone seemed to know where everything should go. One lady even took it upon herself to scrub the path the cows had taken on the cattle drive through the hallway. Finally, the sun began to go down, and our helpers sat on the ground amidst dry grass and sagebrush to rest. Everything was in the house, and while it didn't look like the cover of *Architectural Digest*, I had no idea how so much work had gotten done. Someone had even picked a bouquet of yellow daisies and put them on the cracked mantel over the fireplace. One of the men brought out a guitar from his pickup, and another pulled out his harmonica. As they played, everyone sang, and I marveled at the events of the last two days. I felt out of place so far from the South. I had never known people who acted first and never bothered to ask questions later. I got a preview that night of a certain code of the West: It didn't matter where a person had been or what a person had. It was who he was inside and what kind of a neighbor he was that counted.

"Thank you, Fred, for bringing us to this strange place," I said as he put his arm around my shoulders and tapped his foot to the music. "I want to fit in so badly."

"Just give folks a helpin' hand when they need it, and you'll do fine," he said.

"Darlin'?" I murmured as I nuzzled my lips into the nape of his neck.

"Yeah, what is it, baby?"

"I love our new house and everything, and I think the outhouse with the half-moon carved on the door is cute, but, well, how much longer till you get the toilets hooked up?"

CHAPTER III

Tenting Tonight

I KNEW THAT my new husband was quite a camper. He had grown up all over Montana sleeping in tents and bags, and he counted the days until he could take his new family into the hills with him. Frankly, camping was not a real turn-on for me, but I figured that was because of my unpleasant memories of camping out as a child.

Growing up, during the summers at our farm on Lake Lanier in North Georgia, I camped out because I had to. My parents did not allow me to smoke, look at the pictures of naked people in Dad's magazines, or read dirty books . . . things I felt were mandatory for adolescents. I kept my copy of *Fanny Hill* hidden and carefully guarded the issue of *Tic Toc* I found in the bottom of Dad's bass boat. I found a carton of Viceroy cigarettes there, too, and all my booty went along on my campouts.

I didn't own a tent, so my sleeping bag had to suffice. That meant waking up in the early morning covered in rain or dew. I eventually moved my campsite to the bass boat that had produced my smokes and half my reading matter. I loaded my treasures into it, then covered the whole boat with a large piece of canvas. I would spend hours drifting along, puffing away and reading by flashlight about the escapades of Fanny Hill, which I did not understand but enjoyed because there were a lot of "bad" words. Camping for me was neither a pleasant commune with flora and fauna, nor was it relaxing. It was synonymous with bugs, rain, cold, and unbrushed teeth, which was the worst part of it after smoking a pack of cigarettes the night before.

Following two unsuccessful marriages, I learned the art of compromise . . . smile as sensually as possible for your age, agree with the plan, then do it your way. I lied and told Fred I would be thrilled to go camping with him and the children, but I had a few prerequisites. First, I had to have good food on the trip . . . none of that cowboy stew stuff. I also required bugproof bedding since I hated the thought of ticks and mosquitoes, and, most importantly, it was mandatory that I have access to hot water so that I could successfully implement my daily Erno Laszlo cleansing ritual, which required that I use special oil-removing

soap, then rinse my face thirty times. Fred assured
me that I could camp in luxury, but just to make
sure, I ordered a couple of items out of the L. L.
Bean catalogue: a Blue Ridge Camping Hammock,
which allowed the sleepy camper to zip herself into
a canoe-like swing between two trees, and the Sun
Shower, which produced hot water in three hours
using the collected energy of the sun.

We decided to take the pickup truck instead of
horses since I did not know how to pack a horse for
camping and did not want to learn . . . no horse
could stand still that long. By the time Fred had
finished piling everything in the back of his truck,
it looked like we had been evicted and were
headed to California to hire on as migrant workers.
Bruce was dressed in his usual camouflage gear,
complete with olive green face paint and a camo
headband, a la Rambo. Lisa looked as though she
were headed to the fleshpots of Babylon in her
miniskirt, tank top, hot pink heels, and wide
leather belt, nearly as wide as her skirt. Fred knew
better than to comment. In only ten short months
he had learned never to try and reason with a teenage girl.

We drove on miles of dirt and gravel roads, and
as we began to climb higher into the mountains,
the roads turned into logging trails. We eventually
stopped in a cool forest of spruce and pine with a
sparkling stream nearby that ribboned its way
through raspberry and elderberry bushes. Fred
said it was full of trout, and Lisa, who was humili-
ated to be sharing the outdoor experience with her
family, muttered "Big deal" under her breath.

We began to unload our gear, and everyone was given a job: Fred's was to set up the tent and hang my bed and shower; I was to dig out a campfire site; Lisa's job was to gather firewood and gripe; and Bruce's job, much to his glee, was to dig a latrine. After a couple of hours, as dusk set in, we had a fire going, a tent and my special hammock set up, and some horribly lascivious music blaring from Lisa's sleek lavender battery-operated tape deck. I began to cook hamburgers and hashbrown potatoes while Fred took the rest of our food and hung it in a tree away from the campsite. I had read many stories of campers who kept their food too near their camps, an automatic invitation to bears. I adhered to the same philosophy about scavenger bears that I did about burglars in the city . . . take the food, but don't put me on the menu, too.

As dinner cooked, I pulled out the guitar Fred had given me for my birthday. I knew how to play only three chords, and I still had to look at the little waffle-iron pictures in my book to find those, but sometimes I lucked out and listeners could nearly identify "Greensleeves" or "Scotch and Soda." The kids were not bothered by my music since they were plugged into the tape deck with their headsets, reclining in a languorous state with their heads propped on logs and their feet near the fire. Fred and I sang many songs to the less than melodious strains of my guitar, and somehow the mountains made me feel that the moose and the elk wanted to join in.

Suddenly, I smelled something . . . an unfamiliar and acrid odor. In my self-induced euphony, I had not noticed that the fire had spread and the soles on Lisa and Bruce's tennis shoes were dripping into it. Fred yanked the kids up and all but threw them like javelins, feet first into the stream. In the meantime, I tried to save the handle of the frying pan with the hashbrowns in it, but it, too, slid slowly off into the fire. Luckily, dinner did not taste like plastic or rubber, but the kids were nearly inconsolable over the loss of their Reeboks, which they blamed totally on me and my guitar.

It was decided that Bruce and Lisa would sleep in the tent, Fred wanted to sleep in his sleeping bag by the fire, and I, of course, had Bean's hanging bunk. There was a flashlight by the fire in case anyone had to go to the bathroom in the night, and before turning in, Bruce showed everyone where he had dug the latrine.

Awakened by a blood-curdling scream sometime in the night, I expected the snout of a bear to come ripping through my netting at any moment. I awaited the claws and gnashing of teeth. What I got instead was someone in a frenzy, tearing at the zipper on my covered hammock, then crashing down on top of me, which caused my entire bed to shimmy down the tree and collapse on the ground. Lisa, wood nymph of the mountains, was trying to crawl back into the womb. Fred was standing over us, his loaded .44 pistol drawn, and Bruce was shivering at the tent's door.

"What the hell are you doing, Lisa?" I asked, trying to move out from under her.

"Something was after me . . . an animal came out of a hole and chased me!" she exclaimed.

"What hole? Come show me," Fred said.

Lisa did not budge. "Get that ass Bruce to show you . . . it came out of that pee hole he dug!"

Bruce, whose eyes were the size of billiard balls, said, "She's crazy, Fred. It must have been a dream."

"Probably so, Bruce, but let's go look at your latrine anyway. I'll bring the gun." They went down the trail to Bruce's hole.

A few minutes later I heard a gunshot, and Lisa and I both jumped. Then we heard Bruce laughing.

The boys returned, Bruce still laughing and Fred shaking his head. "Lisa, what exactly happened?" Fred asked.

"Well, I was kinda squatting over that stupid hole, and I heard this kinda scratchy noise inside it, so I jumped up. This nose poked out, and when I started to run, this big like . . . raccoon started chasing me!"

"Well, I'm afraid Bruce was kinda lazy today when he dug you gals a latrine. He found a hole already dug, and he just enlarged it. Only it belonged to a badger first. How'd you like it if somebody peed in your living room?"

"What were you shooting at?" I asked, thoroughly disgusted with Bruce.

"That badger was still hanging around, so I just scared him back inside. Normally, I'd have killed him, 'cause they can be vicious, and they are aggressive. But I just didn't feel right about it, seein' as how he was probably just sittin' down to dinner when all hell broke loose inside his den."

Since Lisa had ripped my hundred-dollar hammock apart, I had to sleep in the tent with her and Bruce, but we insisted that Fred continue to sleep outside by the fire to guard against possible badger retribution.

The next morning I woke up first and faced the odious task of crawling out of my warm sleeping bag and heading down to the stream. It was imperative that I get a pot of water for the coffee and another pot to heat for my thirty rinses, since the sun was not far enough up to have warmed my solar shower. I also decided to brush my teeth while I was at the stream. Trying to lean over the freezing water and balance on two slick rocks with my Indian moccasins was hard enough, but I was also being attacked by some very strange black bugs . . . not like the no-see-ums in the South. These were definitely see-ums, and they liked my eyes and toothpaste-filled mouth best. As I waved my hands around my face trying to swat the bugs away, I turned to climb up the slight embankment out of the water. Just then, I heard a sudden splash downstream. I peeked around the heavy brush bordering the water, and my mouth fell open. I admit that I took the Lord's name in vain, long and loud. Sixty yards downstream was an enormous blackish-brown bear. I knew it wasn't Smokey. He wasn't wearing overalls. He must have smelled me; at least he stood up in the water and started sniffing.

I didn't hang around for him to locate the wearer of the stale Chloe. I dropped the pots and started to slip and slide up the muddy bank, whimpering as I tried to stay low so he couldn't see me over the thick brush and hoping, if he did, he might mistake me for a mud puppy salamander. I heard him crash through the stream and then break through the brush. I reached flat ground and began to run, but I still heard twigs and branches breaking. I panicked. Between our camp and me was a pine tree with low limbs. I jumped on one of them and began climbing. When I got about six feet up, I screamed for Fred. Suddenly, a pine cone conked me on the head, followed by some falling pine needles. Slowly, I turned both eyes upwards until they met in cycloptic union between my eyebrows. About six feet above me in the tree was a pair of black feet with scuffed-up black pads on the bottoms, just like the slippers I had given my dad for Christmas the year before, only twice as big. Our eyes met . . . he went up, and I came down, hitting the ground running.

I met Fred and the kids as I made my way toward the campsite only a few hundred feet away. I was screaming about being attacked by a vicious bear, and Fred cocked his loaded .44 pistol.

"Show me where he went, and you two stay here," he said to Lisa and Bruce, who had not stopped blabbering.

"He's right there!" I said, pointing to the pine tree, which was still moving slightly.

"You mean you chased him up a tree, Mom?" Bruce asked, clearly impressed.

"No! Not on purpose! I didn't know he was up the damned thing! I thought *he* was chasing *me*!" I said hysterically.

"Calm down, honey. That poor bear is much more scared than you are. Let's just leave him alone now, and he'll come down after we leave. He's not gonna hurt anybody."

"No, you have to shoot him before he attacks us!" I yelled.

"Kathy," Fred said patiently, "let's go back to camp, have some coffee, then we'll go catch our breakfast. By the time we get back, that bear will be long gone."

"I'm not going near that stream again!" I declared fervently.

"But, Mom," said Bruce, who was armed with a Chinese star and his Swiss army knife and was vastly disappointed no shots had been fired, "you can't stay at our campsite by yourself. What if the bear comes?"

At that point, Lisa, who had said nothing but "Oh, my God, oh, my God," repeatedly throughout the incident, spoke, "I'm getting out of this totally creeped-up place . . . I cannot *believe* my retarded mother is . . . like, in a tree with a bear, and I could be at Twyla's video party!"

I ignored the teen narrative and decided I had no choice but to follow the kids back to the camp while Fred went down to the stream to collect the coffeepot. I noticed he kept one eye on the bear tree and one hand near his holster as he went.

The guys left to go fishing, and Lisa and I decided to live dangerously and stay in camp after all, mainly because she had to wash her hair, apply her war paint, and begin her sunbathing. I decided to stay because I had the truck to hide in if the bear appeared, and I did not want to catch breakfast in the beast-infested stream. It always looked good when people like John Denver dragged a string of fish over to a grill and tried to sell some gross cereal on television, but any hungry person can attest to the fact that looking at a fish face on a fire first thing in the morning is nauseating . . . I'd rather suck out all the blue and red jelly-looking stripes in my Aqua-Fresh toothpaste and eat that. Nonetheless, Fred and his adoring stepson set off to catch something utterly repulsive for breatkfast. Meanwhile, as I waited for the water for the coffee to boil, I feasted on apples, oranges, and Gruyère cheese. Lisa stuck to her usual diet of Doritos and snack cakes with pink coconut on them.

As we ate, the same horrid bugs I had encountered in the stream appeared, and we realized that we had left our bug spray at home. "No big deal, Mom," said Lisa. "I brought that special aloe oil that Granny gave me at the beach last summer to keep the gnats away . . . that'll work," and she dove into her beauty supply kit, which was never more than six inches from her person and housed more cosmetics than were used on *Dallas, Dynasty, Falcon Crest,* and Tammy Bakker all together. We smeared on the greasy substance, but the bugs continued to swarm. The only difference was that instead of landing and walking on your arms and legs, they skated to a standstill in the thick grease.

"Lisa, this stuff is awful . . . we have to wash it off. Now is a good time to try out the shower, even if the water's not warm yet."

I was happy to learn that my shower worked even without warm water, but I attributed that shortcoming to the fact it was only eight o'clock in the morning. At least I was able to wipe off all the bug bodies stuck to me. I returned to the fire to wash and rinse my face with hot water while Lisa took her shower. I had gone inside the tent to change clothes when I heard, "Oh, this is radically fine!" I looked out the door, and there was Lisa holding my plastic shower bag over the fire. The bottom of my four-ply solar energy bag had melted out, and the silver reflective panel used to boost energy had disappeared, leaving only part of the black absorption panel. All in all, I had nothing left but the sides of a rubber bag and a nozzle, which I felt like douching out the inside of Lisa's head with.

"What in heaven's name are you doing with my shower?" I whispered, trying to remain in control.

Lisa, staring at the bag in bewilderment, said, "Heating this thing up faster so I can wash my hair. I mean, I cannot wash my hair in cold water. But this stupid thing is so cheap, it, like, fell apart!"

"It's rubber! What the hell did you think it was going to do when you held it over a fire?" I asked in a fury.

"Well, I thought it was like some space stuff or something," Lisa said with one of those blank looks that drive mothers to primal scream treatment centers. "Don't get so p.o.'d, Mother, it's just a rubber bag . . . big deal."

Thus far the camping trip had cost me, personally, $114, not to mention the fright factor, and I still had one more night to go.

Fred and Bruce returned about an hour later with four trout, but luckily they were aware of my fisherman's motto: You catch it, you clean it (preferably away from me). Fred showed Bruce how to begin the cleaning process and also how to dispose of the innards so they would not attract bears. While Bruce followed his instructions, Fred began cooking up an enormous breakfast of bacon, eggs, fried potatoes, and the fresh trout. How revolting!

I was busy studying my wildflower books while Lisa was doing her best to emulate her idol, Madonna. She was sunning herself in a Hawaiian print bikini in the back of the pickup and applying a large black mole with a charcoal pencil. When everyone finished eating and dressing for the day, we gathered up our hiking gear and set off to spend the day studying wildflowers. Lisa and I refused to go unless Fred took along his gun, and Bruce voluntarily brought his usual arsenal of Chinese stars, knives, and a slingshot, which Lisa teased him about unmercifully.

"I'm sure you're really gonna kill some bear with that wic-k-k-k-ked slingshot," she said to taunt him.

"Hey, fatty, it worked on Goliath, didn't it? And if you don't shut up, I'm gonna use that fake mole on your lip for target practice." With that, he flipped a pebble at his sister's head.

Our less-than-congenial group took off on our expedition and walked through fields of breathtaking flowers and hills covered with raspberries. When we reached a high ridge overlooking a creek, Fred showed us where to find huckleberries, which were delicious and tasted like wild blueberries. The afternoon was filled with lots of picture taking, wildlife and flower lectures from Fred, and continual bickering by the kids. Throughout the afternoon, I made the solemn vow never to take my teenage daughter into the woods again. She was not designed to walk uphill, and she tripped over every root in her path because she periodically checked her make-up in a mirror that was so large it could have hung in Versailles. She also had her eyes closed much of the time because that's what teenagers do when they groove to the sounds of their Walkman playing such profound songs as "Sexual Healing," "We Don't Have to Take Our Clothes Off (to Have a Good Time)" and my favorite, "Tooth and Nail," by some group with high voices called Dokken. What ever happened to songs like "Sittin' on the Dock of the Bay"?

We returned to our camp at suppertime. Fred had to clean out the campfire and start from scratch since there was enough rubber in our fire pit to mold a spare tire for the pickup. I had splurged and packed steaks, corn on the cob, and for dessert, a special treat, the makings for so-mores. Absolutely no campout was complete without that classic marshmallow-graham cracker-Hershey bar combination, and I had brought plenty. We carefully cleaned all the dishes and put away the trash, then settled down to cook our dessert. I had remembered to bring coat-hangers for the marshmallows, but Bruce refused to use one. He insisted on using a Ramboesque method, whittling his own stick and sticking his marshmallow on the sharp end. On his very first poke into the fire, Bruce's marshmallow ignited, which naturally ignited the stick he was holding. Having some latent pyromaniacal tendencies, Bruce held the flaming torch above the fire and whirled it around like a sparkler. Unfortunately, Lisa, who was plugged into her Walkman and getting down with some mellow music, was in the line of fire when Bruce's marshmallow was flung like a meteor. It hit her square on the side of her head. She was lucky because her earphones caught some of the goo, but the rest of the smoking cinder was mashed in her hair. I have been around professional athletes, sailors, Indians who've had many bottles of MD 20-20, and newspapermen, but never have I heard such a barrage of profanity. I blamed it on Fred's colorful language, but he said he had never even heard a cowboy dragged by his own horse through barbed wire talk like that. He blamed my previous husbands.

I must admit I felt sorry for Lisa. Sticking a hot, drooling marshmallow in a teenage girl's hair would be like telling Aphrodite the zit on her back was oozing through her toga at the Miss World pageant. I tried to pull the sticky mess out of Lisa's head while Fred went to the stream to get a bucket of water so she could wash her hair. Bruce had wisely banished himself to the tent and was pretending to be asleep. Finally, after cleaning Lisa up and negotiating a truce between my two offspring, we got them bedded down in the tent. I removed all of Bruce's weapons. To be on the safe side, Fred invited me to spend the night outside with him since it was such a warm, beautiful night, and I readily agreed. We took our sleeping bags and placed them with our feet at the base of a large pine tree, not too far from the fire. Before we went to sleep, I shared my special stash of peanut chocolate-chip cookies, which I had kept hidden in my pocketbook.

It was two o'clock in the morning when I woke halfway up and felt something walk across the end of my sleeping bag. The fire had all but gone out, so I could not see anything. Still, I knew something had walked across it.

"Fred," I whispered, "wake up!"

"What's the matter? he mumbled.

"Something weird happened . . . I felt something walk across my sleeping bag!"

"It was probably Lisa looking for the ax to dice Bruce up with."

"Come on, I felt it. Where's the flashlight?"

"Over by the fire. I'll get it," and he crawled out of his sleeping bag.

He shined the light all around our sleeping bags and up and down the enormous tree, then said, "My gosh, would ya look at that. Kathy, crawl real slow out of your bag and head for the truck. We gotta bear settin' wide-eyed in our tree."

My body froze. No way was I coming out of that bag. I dove to the bottom of it, quivering.

"Kathy, get out of it," Fred said a bit more anxiously.

"No! Get the gun and let 'im have it!" I said in a muffled whisper.

With that, Fred picked up the end of my sleeping bag and dragged it, with me inside, across the campsite to the pickup. Then he shook me out and loaded me into the front seat. He then went and got the kids out of the tent and put them in the front seat, too. We all sat and watched the bear, who did not move at all for a while. When he came down, we barely made out that he was large, black and had a tag in his ear. Bruce asked Fred if the bear had been branded like the calves that had tags in their ears, and Fred explained that the Fish and Game Department tags some bears because they can be a problem by hanging out at picnic sites and devouring the picnic as well as the picnicker. The tags can help the game wardens identify repeat offenders. They also tag bears in order to follow their migration and study their habits.

As we watched, the bear ambled around the fire and then over to the tent, sniffing madly as he went. He walked through the tent door, collapsing one side of the tent. He just sat inside with the tent hanging on him for what seemed like an hour. Fred cracked the window, but all we could hear were some crunching sounds.

"What is he doing in there?" I asked, still shaking.

"Eating something, I'd guess. Did you kids have any food in there, after I told you to put it all in the cooler for me to hang?" Fred asked suspiciously.

"No, I didn't, Lisa said. "Maybe I did have a bag of Doritos in my pocketbook, though."

Bruce piped up with," All I had was two cans of beanie-weenies in case I got hungry in the night. He wouldn't want those, would he?"

"Bruce, a hungry bear will eat anything, and his sense of smell is so strong, he can smell right through cans, cars, bags, anything," said Fred. "That's why you have to be so careful with food and garbage when you're in the woods."

"I don't know why we came on this stupid trip anyway," Lisa whined. There was silence while the rest of us wondered the same thing.

The bear finally finished whatever he was doing in the tent and moved back over to the bottom of the tree. He began to poke around at something lying on the ground.

"My pocketbook!" I gasped.

The bear gently ripped it open and pulled out the crunched-up bag of remaining cookies, which he ate in one gulp, including the bag. Then he picked something else up off the ground.

"He's got my make-up bag! What's he doing with all my lipsticks?" I muttered in amazement. "My God, he's eating them! I'll be, it's my new fifteen-dollar Chanel lipstick . . . Grape Hyacinth, it smells like grapes!" The bear finished his raid, and after about fifteen minutes, he slowly plodded off into the woods.

Kathy Schmook

We did not get out of the truck immediately because we were all in a state of shock. Fred was the first one to alight. With his loaded gun, he went over to the tree. After he looked around for a minute, he motioned for us to follow. The kids and I hesitantly climbed out.

"Look at this," Fred said, as he held up the remains of my plastic Louis Vuitton pocketbook, which I had paid five dollars for on the Spanish Steps in Rome a couple of years before. "See what can happen if you do not respect the bears and their strong olfactory sense?" he said to me in a very condescending manner.

"Well, Tarzan of Yellowstone, I only know one thing about that damn bear," and I held up my shredded empty lipstick case. "Somewhere in the Rocky Mountains of Montana there is a bear walking around with lips that look like Joan Crawford's in *What Ever Happened to Baby Jane?* !"

As an experienced camper, I can make the following suggestions to the novice:

1. Nature is not free.
2. Camping is not relaxing, at any age.
3. Always pitch your tent in the back of your truck and keep the engine idling.
4. Never take anyone under the age of twenty along, especially if you are related.
5. Unless you can play the guitar like Jose Feliciano, don't bother to take one along.
6. Cooking trout on a campfire does not change their expression or make them any more palatable.

48

7. Makeup, shortie nighties, and bedroom slippers are not necessary.
8. Bears do climb trees . . . and enjoy it.
9. Bears do eat cans and plastic and, on occasion, photographers.
10. It is too nerve-racking to cook outside. I have discovered a campsite only a half-mile from Pizza Hut and Baskin-Robbins, yet still in the mountains. Write for directions. References are required. No one who has ever consumed granola, Tang, or trail mix will be considered.

Kathy Schmook

CHAPTER IV

Flakes

ONE OF THE factors in my decision to move west was that I would be able to enjoy winter sports regularly. I was especially eager to resume downhill skiing. I had skied on and off for the past twenty years, but it had been mainly off for two reasons: one, Stone Mountain, the only real hill in Atlanta, didn't get a lot of snow. Besides, a devoted Southerner could hardly ski over the faces of Stonewall Jackson, Jefferson Davis, and Robert E. Lee, which are carved on its side. Two, none of my previous husbands had liked to ski. So, when a well-meaning friend or relative called to invite us on a ski trip, instead of telling the truth about Dilbert's preferring to stay home and practice his jai alai shots, I dutifully told them we were busy perfecting our Lamaze breathing in case of pregnancy.

Actually, one of my husbands did try to ski once, but he was nearly killed in a spectacular accident that longtime residents of Vail, Colorado, still recall with a tremble. He refused to take any lessons when we went on our one and only ski trip. Therefore, he never learned to stop, slow down or turn. On the very first run of the day, my husband, henceforth known as Lightning, rode the chairlift to the top of the highest peak, fell off the lift, taking me with him, and began a death-defying descent with such velocity he was airborne at times. He ended up at the bottom of an advanced slope on a funnel-shaped trail that jet-propelled him across a straightaway and into the village. Since he could not turn, much less stop, he skied into someone's garage, where they were barbecuing pork chops. He cracked three ribs and suffered severe burns on his face and neck. One pork chop burned a tattoo on his chest in the shape of Oklahoma. We never skied together again.

Unfortunately, the next time I skied was years later, after a divorce. I went with a bunch of women to lick my wounds, and my skiing then was quite different. I had never been a showoff before, especialy since it was hard to do tricky things while mastering the snowplow, but on the singles trip, I skied with reckless abandon! All newly divorced people do things they would never do under ordinary circumstances, and I was no exception. I took many lessons, determined to perfect my parallel style and to have a legal reason to stare at the back of my instructor's pants. I had never noticed before, but there was something about the rear end of an Austrian in stretch pants that defied description. He skied down slopes in front of me and said to follow close behind in his tracks. No problem, I'd have followed him off the face of Mt. McKinley with the eternal hope of a rear-end collision.

Now, I don't have to worry about learning to ski again or about having a place to ski. I live in an area where ski resorts abound, and I have even mastered the lift so that I no longer fall off. Well, sometimes I still have accidents, but at least I've learned how to make them look like the other person's fault. But skiing is a different sport than it was when I skied so sporadically before.

For one thing, the equipment is different. The boots are more comfortable and are no longer designed and built by Herman Munster. I was also delighted to learn that it is no longer a necessity to wear skintight pants. There is nothing quite as miserable as falling on the side of a mountain in tight britches and trying to get back up while the waistband is slicing the top part of your body in two, not to mention what the seam between the legs is doing. Fortunately, the slice-and-dice design has become dated. Experts in Europe engaged in studies on women over the age of forty and discovered they were able to hold their stomachs in only while standing up, not while lying down in snow. It seemed the aristocratic ladies complained about the number of rolls that were instantly visible upon falling . . . especially if one were unfortunate enough to fall in the lift line or, God forbid, in front of a dining chalet. Therefore, the designers came out with looser and bulkier ski apparel. Today, some of the jumpsuits even have rubber wet suits hidden on the inside that act like a girdle! Hallelujah! Let the hips fall where they may! Finally, no more gab about the flab showing in the old Stretch Armstrong suits.

Another thing about skiing that has changed is that I now have the pleasure of skiing downhill with my two children. Sometimes it is a pleasure. Other times it is a nightmare. Now I have witnesses to report on my prowess, and they do . . . to anyone that will listen. On the negative side, they add to the time factor. By the time Lisa has decided what ski sweater and turtleneck with matching eyeshadow she is going to wear, I am already exhausted from bending over and adjusting the buckles on my boots. Bruce, the ever nattily attired rogue that he is, takes only a moment to don his ski attire, which is the basic camouflage suit with a ninja twist: he ties a headband around his head and carries a pair of numchucks over his shoulder. The usual arsenal of Chinese stars, survival knife, and cherry bombs is hidden elsewhere. The kid would be worth thousands to the Contra rebels and is probably under contract to Ollie North.

Recently, the children and I went skiing at Big Sky, a wonderful ski resort near where we live. When we went to rent skis the first morning, we had to fill out the perfunctory questionnaires regarding rental. They asked about height, weight, shoe size, age, color of eyes, mother's maiden name, smoking preference, prior felony convictions and if a convicted felon, any plans you might have for ripping off the rental skis. My daughter, Lisa, drooled over my arm as I carefully filled out my form and, in a resounding voice, said, "Oh sure, Mom. That's not what you weigh! The man told me to put down my real weight or my skis might not come off when I fall, and I could break my leg."

That will be after I break your mouth, I thought to myself.

By the time we had all three rented our skis and bought lift tickets, and I had doled out lunch money, I could have bought a new car for what I'd spent. I began to wonder if skiing with the kids was worth it.

After studying a trail map, they took me up a lift they told me was awesome. Naturally, they did not ride in the chair with me because Lisa was on her never-ending quest for boys, and, for Bruce, in his camouflaged "No Guts, No Glory" T-shirt, a trip up the lift with Mom would have been totally degrading. On the way up, one of the strange phenomena about Montana weather occurred . . . the wind came from out of nowhere and began blowing about fifty miles an hour. A bit unsettling on land, however, it is downright murderous if you are hanging from a cable and dangling over precipices eighty feet below. To make matters worse, the lift stopped, and the wind blew my seat sideways so that I was parallel to the ground. There was no doubt in my mind that I would never live through this ordeal. As I swung helplessly in the chair, I seriously eyed the nearest spruce tree and began to plan my jump in case the cable snapped. I also made all the solemn vows I usually make in emergencies: no more cussing, even in private, no more beer drinking at the saloon after Bible study, no more staring at the Salvation Army ladies' shoes and snickering, and I would definitely get "Will the Circle Be Unbroken" down pat on my guitar.

After what seemed to be an eternity, we arrived at the top, and Lisa reapplied her make-up and checked her hair while Bruce asked with a smirk, "Hey, Lisa, how'd you like riding up with mogul face? Did he put his arm around you?" He was referring to the Oxy-10 poster boy Lisa had shared the ride with.

She took a pole and swatted him on the back. "At least I didn't cry when the wind was blowing hard, goob brain!"

I interrupted at that point, "OK, that's enough. Where to, you guys?" With a final obscene gesture directed at Lisa (at least I hoped it was final), Bruce led us down a path to the top of a slope. I looked over the edge, and it was so steep the bottom curled back underneath and was not visible.

"Forget it, Bruce," I said. "I do not ski black diamonds (advanced slopes) . . . remember Mom's knees." Knees always seemed to be a good reason to get out of any undesirable athletic feat. Actually, the only time I ever hurt my knees was the year before when I stepped out of the car in front of Pizza Hut and slipped and fell on a sheet of ice. I landed with a thonk on both hands and knees. Much to my dismay, the children were with me. "Look, Lisa, Mom's a pony — let's ride her," Bruce exclaimed with no respect. I hoped the patrons inside Pizza Hut could not read my lips as I assailed my merciless children.

"Come on, Mom," Lisa whined, "let's, like, go now . . . I've seen lots of old ladies go down this one. It has a few bumps only at the bottom." With that vote of confidence, she and her brother took off down the slope.

I had two choices: either sidestep back up the hill and walk over to the next slope or try to ski slowly down the forbidding one in front of me, knowing if I ever lost control and took the brakes off, I'd end up in Wyoming. I practiced the deductive reasoning I had learned a few years earlier while living in the urban jungle and taking a Creative Mugging course designed to turn all muggings into positive experiences. I excelled in the class. The instructor told me he thought I must have been a guard on a rapid transit system in another life since I advocated the bearing of arms on all public and private means of transportation, including taxis and rental car shuttles. However, I dropped out when the teacher refused to let me give my demonstration on how to turn a Kirby vacuum cleaner into a semi-automatic weapon.

I reflected on what I had learned and asked myself, "What is the worst thing that could happen if I ski down the slope, and is the challenge worth it?" The worst thing was the possibility of breaking a bone, which at my age would probably be a hip. Then I would have to forfeit the dance lessons Fred had won for us at the rattlesnake-eating contest at the fair. But the challenge seemed worth it since there was a little pub near the bottom of the slope that sold divine baby-back ribs and hot spiced wine.

I aimed myself downhill and took off. The first twenty yards were not bad, but then the moguls appeared. I realized Lisa had given me false information. Not only was the slope covered with the snowy bumps, but there was also a lift that ran its entire length. Nothing is more demeaning than falling and subsequently wallowing under a lift full of skiers. The voices of the riders carry, and it is not unusual to hear comments from overhead like, "Wonder why she was on that slope anyway?" or "She must have gotten separated from that Amway convention out here." I'd heard it all before. I resorted to the ploy I normally used in such situations, whereby I purposely stopped under the lift and pretended to adjust a buckle on my boot. In reality I was peering out from underneath my goggles to plot the easiest way down. I decided the only way to avoid the humiliation of becoming a human snowball and rolling down the slope was to traverse (ski sideways) back and forth the whole way down.

That did not work. After my first trip across the slope, I realized the moguls were definitely impeding my progress. I'd ski up one side of the bump, stop on top, the ski backwards right back down. Sometimes I got stuck between two moguls with the toes of both skis in one and the heels in another, the center of the skis in midair.

I looked through the trees at the edge of the slope while I was trying to get up enough nerve to negotiate a turn. I realized if I skied through the woods I might end up on a less difficult slope. I started the rather arduous trek but got only about six feet into the forest when both skis completely disappeared. I had never been in snow so deep it ate your legs, but before I knew it, I was thigh-high in the stuff. I inched my numb fingers and arms down through the snow to try to release the skis, but they would not come off. Trying to walk through four feet of powdery snow in skis was like trying to swim the English Channel with Paul Prudhomme on one leg and my ex-husbands on the other. I had to half crawl, half tunnel my way through, but it was worth it in the end. Even though it too had a lift over it, the slope I ended up on was much easier than the other one had been, and I heaved a sigh of relief as I started down.

As luck would have it, my two little darlings had been able to ski down, ride the lift back up and somehow end up skiing on *my* hill. As I made my way rhythmically down the slope, with a high degree of agility and grace, I might add, I heard, "Golly, Mom, how'd you end up on this baby hill? We saw you go into the woods, but Lisa said you were just going to the bathroom." Then Bruce and his sister did a series of tricky zigzag turns right in front of me that caused me to fall and ski down the rest of the mountain on my back with my legs whirling overhead. Above me, the riders on the lift didn't even try to stifle their derision.

"Hey, Mom, far out fall," Bruce said, as I dug the snow out of my bib overalls. "You looked like Air Wolf!"

That did it. I sent them off to ski alone, and I headed for the pub. I knew then it was time to investigate the allure of the après-ski life at closer range. Perhaps I'd purchase some high-fashion ski clothes, some mysterious goggles with pictures of Vanna White on the sides, and a big furry hat with matching boots, then just sit around in the sun sipping hot drinks and talking about my last trip to Gstaad.

The Skinny Skis

Most of the new friends I made out West convinced me that I was spending too much time worrying about downhill skiing. They suggested I try cross-country skiing since it was much less expensive and because all I had to do was walk out of my front door and start skiing. The only thing I knew about what I thought of as flat-land skiing was that it ranked over swimming as the number one overall conditioning exercise. To me, that meant that it must be excruciatingly painful. However, I had seen one of the Virginia Slims ads with a fairly unathletic-looking girl dressed in cross-country garb so I decided it couldn't be that hard if you could smoke and ski, too.

So, in an unceasing effort to stave off the effects of an approaching midlife body strike (condition where entire figure gives up and drops three inches), I threw myself and my partner by wedlock, the mysterious Fred, into a new adventure using the skinny skis. For Christmas that year, I gave us both a pair of skis, which I found on sale. For only thirty dollars a set, we each got plastic skis, a pair of weird-looking shoes, and some long poles. I hadn't spent that much on a Christmas present for a husband since the time I bought one of them a special meat compressor . . . guaranteed to turn anything even resembling meat into Spam. He didn't appreciate it either; he gave it to the AMVETS truck when it came by, the ungrateful dolt. But I splurged on the skis, and Fred was delighted, especially when I assured him that excessive skiing and the resulting perspiration caused hair growth. However, neither of us was sure about exactly what to do with our new toys, so we headed down to Yellowstone Park for lessons and a day of skiing.

Our teacher was an older German man who did not seem to realize that old dogs are slow to learn new tricks. Actually, he seemed to be a very cruel man. He would not let us use our poles, and he made us spend hours skiing on one ski. Fred asked him if he had ever worked in Auschwitz. For that, Fred had to ski up a hill with one arm tied behind him. However, in Hans's defense, I began to realize he was trying to teach us the importance of changing weight completely from one ski to the other, almost like skating. He showed us how the shoulders naturally followed along as the arms swung the poles one at a time, in front, then in back. Gradually, a certain rhythm developed. As I tried to copy the little bounce Hans put in each step, the song "Side By Side" came to me. It just sort of fit the big walking steps . . . "Oh, we ain't got a barrel of mo-ney" . . . I had it! Suddenly, I realized I had stumbled onto the secret of cross-country skiing — ski on one ski at a time (don't worry about the one in back popping up, it may or may not); then, as the weight is shifted from leg to leg and the shoulders go up and down, the skier should visualize some fruity vaudevillian entertainer and hum "Side By Side." Nothing to it.

After Hans dismissed us with a hopeless smile, Fred and I practiced what we had learned in our lesson on some flat areas and a few very gradual inclines. Hans had taught us how to slow down and stop by using a snowplow technique, so, after a while, we decided to become more adventurous and ski a trail that wound its way through some woods and up a mountainside. We quickly realized that one of the beauties of cross-country skiing was being surrounded by a certain stillness and solitude. There was a sense of oneness with nature, with the only sounds being those of the skis breaking through snow or of deer waiting until we were surprisingly close and darting into the timber.

As we skied further along the woodland trail, we noticed we were gradually climbing. At some points where there was a switchback (hairpin) turn, I lost control and nearly skied backwards into Fred. For some strange reason, neither of us realized that what goes up, must come down . . . and probably fast, too. We continued to climb higher and higher, and as the trail became icy in places, we were forced to take off our skis and walk.

"Kathy," Fred said with a bit of trepidation, "don't you think we'd better turn around and start down? It's getting hard to even walk up this mountain."

"We can't turn back now," I said, with the true grits of my collard green ancestry. "We're almost at the top. Think of how much fun it will be to ski down . . . we can just relax."

I rounded the final bend in the trail and came to a knoll, which ended our climb. We took a breather and shared the mineral water and apples Fred had brought in his backpack. It was almost the Last Supper.

"You go first," I offered magnanimously to my new husband, who usually obeyed me since he was still in the yearling stage of our marriage.

"OK, but how do we turn around those sharp switchbacks?" my honeybunch asked with understandable consternation.

"Just remember what Hans said about using the snowplow to slow down and turn," I replied. "And never forget the power of prayer," I added under my breath.

Off he went, with me close behind. Fred's skis made a *swoosh* sound as he missed the first turn without even the chance to attempt it. It was so sharp and steep that he went right over the edge, sailed through a little clearing, and landed with an upright thud on the trail below. I didn't have time to laugh. Although I made the switchback turn, I skied around it so fast that I ran into Fred, who had taken the shortcut, and caught him from the Brooklyn side. We ended up in a pile of skis and flailing poles.

"Why were you just standing here like a dummy? Why didn't you get out of the way?" I yelled in exasperation.

"Where the hell should I be, since I just landed and I'm still trying to get my ankles out of my jawbone!" Fred said in a fury.

We continued to mutter at each other as we examined our minor injuries and got ready to take off again.

"We'll give you the red badge of courage this time, and you can go first," Fred said as he snapped his ski shoe back into place.

"OK, I will, but if you see me stop or slow down, don't come plowing into the back of me!" Down the trail I went. I picked up speed rapidly, and the carved scales on the bottoms of my skis did little to slow me up. I made the next turn all right, but I saw a steep downgrade ahead. I knew I wouldn't make it. On the right side of the trail was a snowbank about ten feet high, and I aimed for it, thinking it would be a safe landing site. As I skied into it, the ends of my skis went in only about eight inches, then hit something solid. What a jolt! My face was launched into the bank and out again while my entire body was a study in reverberation. I felt like a tuning fork. Fred was a mere blur as he flew around the turn on one leg of a snowplow and passed me. I desperately dug myself out of the bank.

I attempted a slow start down the trail once again and heard lots of sticks breaking, then cursing, so I knew Fred had met his demise somewhere nearby. Sure enough, off to the side a few yards further down, Fred was looped over a log and looked as though he was waiting for the proctologist to arrive.

"What are you doing hanging on that log?" I had to ask with a smirk.

"The same thing you were doing stuck in that snowbank," a very disgruntled Fred answered. "I'm taking these damn skis off and shoving them up Hans's Wiener schnitzel!" He jerked both skis off and began walking.

We made an interesting couple as we hobbled down the trail. Fred on foot and me perfecting my crash-and-go technique. After one of my agonizing falls, I heard Fred yell, "Hey! I've got it!" Down he came, sailing past me on a sled he had made out of his skis. He still didn't make it around the turns too well, but at least he didn't have as far to fall. He had placed his skis side by side so that they touched, then sat back over his feet and held the backs of the skis together. I tried it and instantly decided it was easier than trying to negotiate the trail standing up. We continued sledding down the rest of the trail.

We were almost at the end and had just completed a series of dipsy-doodles when Fred ran over a hidden branch and wiped out. I went past him on my sled at breakneck speed as I approached the final downhill. I gasped when I saw three cow elk straddling the trail while they pawed at the snow, looking for food underneath. I heard Fred yelling from behind me, "Don't hit 'em, they'll stomp you!" I wondered how I was supposed to slow down!

I got closer and closer, and it appeared that I was going under the belly of one of the elk.

"Move!" I heard myself scream absurdly to the animals. I zoomed by as they lazily stepped aside. I finished in a blaze of glory by sledding down to the main road and running over the only two-foot pine tree around. A couple of Japanese tourists were parked on the road astride snowmobiles and seemed to be enjoying the show as they applauded, laughed and took photos. Fred came barreling down to the finish and ran over the exact same tree.

"Wasn't that great?" I said in a loud voice to Fred, pretending we had planned the near elk collision.

"You bet," he said convincingly, as he picked the pine needles out of his zipper. "But next time, let's not even take those dumb poles."

"What poles?" I asked without moving my lips.

We both looked around at the same time and realized we had left our poles back up the trail at the ski/sled conversion point. There was but one quick solution. Fred said, "Tell you what, you go ask Ski-doo over there to let us borrow his snowmobile. Tell him you'll let him borrow your computer skis — the ones that track elk."

The Japanese couple did let us borrow a snowmobile to retrieve our poles, and all we had to do was take twenty-four pictures of them getting on and off their snowmobiles.

The Gay Blade

I decided I might have more luck ice skating. Ever since the days my grandmother took me to see Holiday on Ice at the old Atlanta Auditorium, I wanted to strap on the blades and glide across the ice. I did not want to be Mickey Mouse or Goofy either. I wanted to be one of the graceful ice ballerinas that wore the skimpy chiffon costumes with sequins on them, the ladies that were lifted high in the air by handsome, Adonis-like men in tight, glittery pants and short bolero vests.

As I got older, the fascination continued when I'd watch Sonja Henie spin around with a Bic pen tied onto her skate. I never knew if it was an ad for geriatric skating or for one hell of a writing pen. And then came the beauty and style of Peggy Fleming. Every young girl wanted to emulate her, and when Dorothy Hamill appeared on the scene, nearly every young girl did copy her haircut.

When I was growing up, ice skating in Atlanta was about as popular as downhill skiing in Kansas. It wasn't until a group of aspiring entrepreneurs brought professional hockey to town that we even had a rink. Then they seemed to spring up everywhere.

I was very disappointed the first time I tried to skate, but I decided my clumsiness was because I had weak ankles because I had broken one of them as a child. When I was in fifth grade, I jumped off my grandmother's garage at the prodding of my cousin, Monroe "You Show Me Yours, I'll Show You Mine" Taulman. He had convinced me that I was able to fly because I had eaten three bowls of Jets cereal for breakfast. The advertisement on television claimed it made you *Jet-Propelled*, and it showed some kids on the front of the box soaring into the air. So I jumped and fell like an anvil to the earth, landing cross-legged on top of both feet. I did not know my ankle was broken until a few hours later when my foot popped the laces on my red Keds and a purple egg appeared on the top of my foot.

I tried to skate only one more time while I lived in the South, when I was forced to chaperone at a birthday party one of my children attended. I was sorry to see I had not improved one bit, for I still skated on the inside of my ankle bones with both skate blades stuck out to either side. I spent the entire afternoon gripping the handrail or crashing into some unsuspecting kid.

How ironic that years later I ended up living in a place where ice skating is done on local creeks or ponds and that my children would put ice skates as number one on their Christmas lists. One bright winter afternoon, Lisa, Bruce, and their friend Sara asked me to take them to a nearby creek to skate. I said yes, on the condition that Sara would teach me to skate, too.

"Mom, you can't skate," Lisa announced matter-of-factly. "Remember Lucinda's birthday party that time . . . when you fell on Taffy and smushed her arm and broke her watch?"

"I did not break her watch on purpose. Besides, she was too young to be wearing a Rolex . . . ten years old, a mere guppie (childlike yuppie). Plus, she shouldn't have been skating backwards around me. If she'd looked where she was going, I never would have crashed into her."

"It's OK, Mrs. Schmook," Sara said compassionately. "You can come, and I'll teach you some radical moves . . . even backwards."

"Hope you're wearing a Timex, Sara," Lisa smirked, "so it can take a lickin' and keep on tickin'!"

"Look, John Cameron Swayze, you want to skate or not? Now y'all get your stuff together and let's go." I'd had enough verbal sparring with my daughter.

Lisa insisted on bringing her ghetto-blaster for mood skating with all of her Phil Collins and Madonna tapes. I suddenly remembered the mesmerizing tape young Bruce had given me for Christmas . . . *Great Love Waltzes of All Time*. He had ordered it from the television and the songs were performed by none other than Zamfir and his Pan Flute (I think he's the Slim Whitman of Switzerland). Bruce thrilled to the sounds of "Love

Theme from Romeo and Juliet," "Blue Danube,"
and "The Skater's Waltz," and the thoughtful
young lad ordered it for his mother. I stuck the tape
in my pocket, and after Lisa finished pulling
bunny fur from her muff off her wet manicure, we
left.

We arrived at the picturesque creek, which was
frozen solid. The kids put on their skates, and I
carefully laced my borrowed ones as tightly as possible, hoping to avoid shaky ankles. Sara and Lisa
floated over the ice gracefully, practicing their turns
and spray stops, as they called them (that is, a turn
where the skater is aimed in one direction, then
abruptly jumps sideways, thus stopping and spray-
ing a stream of ice crystals into the air . . . it makes
a sound like fingernails on a blackboard). Bruce
patrolled the creek banks for rocks to play hockey
with, and I merely practiced standing without having my ankles turn in. Sara and Lisa came and
stood on either side of me and helped me get my
balance. After a while, I was actually able to turn
in a small circle and stop gradually without falling.

The kids got bored with skating in one spot, so
they decided to skate upstream and look for a new
area. Since I had never skated *au naturel* before
(i.e., outdoors), I was not aware of varying ice con-
ditions. I quickly learned what to be on the lookout
for: crusty ice pieces that look like somebody
dropped a Sno-Cone mean bumpy ride coming up;
little teeny bubbles under the surface of solid-look-
ing ice means weak ice and feet will be submerged
shortly; long skinny cracks in the ice dispel the

myth that "No man is an island" — beware, the skater will soon be on a floating island.

The trip up the creek was so breathtaking it would have captured the attention of even Currier and Ives. The sunlight hit tiny snow and ice crystals on the frozen creek and in the tree branches that dipped lazily out over the creek bank. It looked like someone had shaken up a glass snow scene souvenir from Austria and it had exploded, throwing minuscule prisms of sparkling color everywhere. I was fascinated to see that six deer eyed us surreptitiously as they hid among the evergreens. They were overwhelmed with curiosity and did not feel threatened enough to run away. I went through a series of knee drops, not unlike those of Jackie Wilson, as I encountered crusty ice patches, but the pain was worth it . . . ice skating at the Omni in Atlanta had never been like what I was experiencing.

We reached a wide area in the creek, and Sara began her efforts to teach me to skate backwards by making me weave my feet in and out, in and out. By cracky, I was just beginning to get the hang of it, when down I went . . . on my cracky. I hit so hard I saw little dots, and I immediately got a terrible headache. Naturally, the kids guffawed.

"What happened?" Lisa giggled.

"I'm laying an egg . . . what does it look like happened? I hit some of that crunchy ice, and it tripped me!" I moaned in agony.

"Are you all right?" Sara asked.

"I guess so, but I landed on *that* bone . . . the coccyx, I think. Let's go back down to where the ice is smoother."

As we skated back to where we had started, I spied one lone deer out of the corner of my eye, and he was staring at me . . . almost smirking. "You'll get yours next hunting season, Flag," I said under my breath.

By the time we reached our starting point, my headache had subsided, and I was ready to practice my backwards skating again. I persuaded Bruce to put on my waltz tape performed by Europe's crown jewel, Zamfir, with his ever-trusty flute. I became lost in a fantasy as I skated to the strains of "The Skater's Waltz." I closed my eyes and envisioned myself leaping, whirling, and touching my nose to my knee as I raised one semi-cellulitic leg in the air behind me. One must never close one's eyes while skating on a woodland brook. I got a little carried away with the moment and skated too close to the edge of the creek. By the time my eyes had opened and I realized what was happening, my skates went straight into some crunchy ice. It threw me on my tippy toes, which I had to stay on to keep my balance, and I had to run faster and faster on point to keep from falling. I kept going even when I left the ice and ran onto the dirt. I was still on my toes, running like an upright Slinky until I hit a root, then . . . "Splonk!" I made a very abrupt stop, again. Fortunately, I did not have an audience.

Walking on the earth is difficult in skates, but I made it back to the creek, where the kids were engaged in a game of hockey with Madonna blaring in the background. "I'll give it one more try," I thought to myself, "just practice my turns a little."

I began some very slow turns, nothing fancy, and the music got louder. I found myself getting the beat suddenly, and before I knew it, I was almost dancing. I had never listened to the words of rock music because it seemed to be nothing but repetitive chortling. Now I heard something about "Papa don't preach." I assumed, naturally, Madonna objected to her father's being a minister. I was combining some backwards turns with some tricky spins when I caught words like, "I've made up my mi-nd, I'm keeping my ba-by!"

"Good heavenly horsefeathers!" I said out loud. "What sort of trash is that?" And then more, "Papa don't preach, I'm in love . . ." With that, I decided on a finale which consisted of a spray stop aimed at the blaster on the edge of the ice. I didn't quite pull it off. My legs went out from under me at the same time. That meant that my entire frame fell from a height of five feet, seven inches with no break in the middle. I landed on the same bone I had hit earlier in the day.

Lisa had to drive us home. I could not sit on my bone, so they laid me out in the back of the pickup and rested my rear end in the spare tire . . . like the doughnuts they give to hemorrhoid sufferers, only on a larger scale. Fred was somewhat alarmed when the truck pulled into the driveway, and three kids, whose ages altogether did not total his, were the only ones in the cab.

"Where's your mom?" he asked frantically.

"She's in the back . . . she hurt her butt," Lisa said, stifling a grin for everything she was worth.

"Yeah," Bruce chimed in, "she's suffering the agony of defeat."

Fred climbed in the back of the truck with me and said tenderly, "Honey, what are you doing in that tire?"

I choked through the tears. "I fell on the ice, and I can't sit down."

Somewhere through a maze of pain I heard a duet singing, "She can't sit down, she can't sit down . . ."

Fred wasted no time. He dumped the three kids (two of them still singing) out and drove me to the emergency room, where X-rays showed I had indeed cracked my coccyx.

"Will I walk again?" I asked the doctor, who seemed bemused by the fact Fred had carried me into the examining room.

"Oh, yes, you'll walk, you just might not sit for a while."

"Well, I guess if Mr. Ed can sleep standing, so can I," and Fred carried me back out to the truck.

"Get me my tire, please, Fred. I'll just sit on it here in the front seat."

"Honey, you can't, you'll be taller than the cab."

"Oh, I don't care, just stick me in the back. I'm in too much pain to argue."

On the twenty-five-mile drive home, I seemed to drift in and out of delirium. There must be a message in the injuries I was sustaining during my first winter out West. I ultimately decided that I was living life as if someone were going to appear one day and say, "OK. Time's up! Time to go back to the city! Hope you've done everything out here you wanted to, 'cause you're headed back to shrinks, debts, and exhaust fumes!"

I just hope it's not the same dude that talks to Oral Roberts.

Kathy Schmook

CHAPTER V

Ladies, Start Your Engines

I AM A RUNNER. I am not a jogger. Joggers run when they feel like it, weather permitting; runners do it because it is an addiction. Joggers run around on their tiptoes in smooth-looking pastel velour suits and forty-dollar aerobic shoes; runners wear whatever restricts them least—the briefest possible pants, a faded T-shirt, and seventy-five-dollar running shoes that resemble heavy earth-moving equipment.

I have no hesitation about confessing that I have never won a race in the fourteen years I have been running. Occasionally, I have lucked out and received a ribbon for finishing in my age group, but I have consistently finished in the bottom half of any field I ran in. I have kept my interest by never letting the competition spoil the sport for me. I don't care if I win. I'm the only person I have ever enjoyed competing against. An entire wall in my home is designated my "Wall of Shame"; on it are the pictures that record my failure to win anything . . . except pity for my age.

I have lost races all over the world. I was in a race once in Athens, Georgia, with a bunch of students from the university, and I finished dead last. That was the only time I recall the refreshments' being removed before the last runner (me) crossed the finish line. I had to hitchhike to the Varsity's Athens branch to get an orange drink. I also finished last in a race in Brisbane, Australia, where a former husband of mine was speaking to a Rotary Club. I could have done much better except that the race was run through a park full of eucalyptus trees with an enormous water slide at the end. The object was to run ten grueling kilometers through the park in the hot sun, then end by jumping on the top of the slide and finishing in a splash at the bottom.

Unfortunately, the park was known for its collection of tame koala bears that lived in the eucalyptuses, and as I ran through, I could not resist stopping and trying to lure the fuzzy little bears down from their perches. I was simply dying to hug one. I finished so late that not only had everyone gone home, but, unbeknownst to me, the water slide had been turned off. When I made my final lunge onto the top of the slide, I had a dry run to the finish with only the bears and a gentle-hearted trash collector looking on. The latter gave me directions for the long walk back to my hotel.

I ran for sheer enjoyment and a sense of accomplishment. I liked to practice the self-discipline of depriving myself of a Sara Lee cherry cheesecake and going out for a quick seven or eight miles instead.

After I had been running for about nine years, I decided I needed to take on a little challenge in my running career, so I set my sights on a marathon. I picked the one in Boston, feeling that if I started at the top, I would never have to worry about working my way up. Besides, I knew my legs, highlighted with lightning bolts of varicose veins, only had one twenty-six-miler in them. I had no intention of actually beating anyone in the race, but I was determined to finish in under four hours. I had a friend who agreed to run it with me, and we trained together diligently—nothing came before our running schedules. We were pictures of dedication and vigor as we both finished the race in well under four hours. Our rigorous training had paid off, and by finishing the onerous race, I realized that anything in life is attainable if you are willing to work hard enough to achieve it. I figured I had conquered the Beast of Boston, what else was there? I moved to Montana and found out.

The mountains gave me a such a feeling of exhilaration that I could not help but begin running again. The hills of the West couldn't be any tougher than those of Atlanta. After all, I had run the infamous Peachtree Road Race with its oppressive heat on the Fourth of July for ten years in succession.

At first I was content to run up and down a dirt road near my house, but eventually I began to feel like I was on a treadmill. The old yearning for some sort of a new challenge returned. At the same time, I received a letter from my mother, referring to the fact that, from the Christmas card with a family photo I had sent her, she was happy to see I had gained some weight, and she complimented me on my attractive matronly figure. The kiss of death. Whenever a mother or a grandmother tells you that your weight is right, not to mention calling you a matron, you know that you have finally reached the finals in the Aunt Bea of Mayberry look-alike contest. First prize, a box of Depend undergarments.

I had to do something. What new feat could I strive toward? One day I was in town at the five-and-ten-cent store looking for some ribbon to braid my horse's mane with. I noticed a sign advertising a race in Trident, a nearby town. It was called the John Colter Run, and it was a cross-country race that covered rugged terrain. In the last two hundred yards, you had to ford the Gallatin River, which was supposed to be knee deep. It was a commemorative race in honor of John Colter's capture and narrow escape from the Indians. According to the legend, after being caught, Colter was stripped of everything, including his shoes, and given a head start by the Indians. He was told that if he was able to outrun them, they would spare his life. Supposedly the race course included some of the famous ground Colter covered. That was it! I had found my new goal.

I asked around, and no one seemed to know much about the run's degree of difficulty. I knew it was seven miles and that I had to get wet at the end, but I never found any actual previous participants to chat with. My husband, who claimed matrons turned him on in a primitive sort of way, did not understand my quest. Since he was familiar with the general topography of the area around the race site, he suggested I do some training in the hills around our house. I took his advice and began training. I ran up the hills, I ran down the hills, and when I got too tired to run, I walked them. I tripped over rocks, waded through creeks, and skidded in cowpies. Finally, the day of the race arrived.

We arrived early at the park where the race began, and it felt good to have the old butterflies back. I anticipated no problem with the seven-mile jaunt through the sagebrush. My husband called me over to a map just as a warning whistle blew.

"Kathy," he said, with his face and brow wrinkled like a bulldog's, "according to this map, there are some really long and steep hills on this course. You be careful, you really aren't used to runs like this."

The audacity of Fred's speaking to me, ex-Boston Marathoner par excellence, with such a lack of confidence irritated me. I said, "Hey, Fred, cool out. This one's in the bag. Old "keg legs" ain't done yet . . . you just worry 'bout having the Coors out when I zip over that finish line." And I dashed away to get in line.

There was no whistle to begin the race. The starter said that the race would begin the way Colter's probably had . . . I hoped they'd send a naked man out in front, but instead someone shot a flaming arrow into the air, and with lots of Indian warwhoops, we were off! I started off in the front of the crowd but very quickly found myself in the middle. No problem. I usually waited to make my move at about mid-distance. I overheard some of the runners saying "save up," and "get ready," and I wondered what they were talking about. I didn't wonder long. In front of me, a sort of bottleneck had formed under a wooden bridge, and people seemed to be waiting in line. I passed under the bridge and was forced to stop. At the same time my eyes followed a bunch of runners in front of me up a cliff . . . a cliff so high that the top of it blotted out the sun. It was so narrow and steep, the runners were walking up, single file. I did not have time to jockey for position because I was caught up in the crowd and forced to begin the climb. At first it was easy to keep up with the person in front of me because he was a big fat man in baggy Bermuda shorts, a Hawaiian shirt, and glasses held on by an elastic strap with pink palm trees on it. He was wearing a hat that said "Fatty" on it. But after he lost his footing and skidded down the hill behind me, there was a space in front of me, and I knew I had to catch up. The novelty was gone at that point. People began passing me on the steep incline, and all I could do was hope that by some miracle all of us might turn into baby elephants and then I would be able to grab hold of the tail in front of me. The pain became unbearable. My calves felt like someone had put a vice grip on them, and the worst part was that I had not gone even a mile yet. I looked up. I still did not see the top of the cliff. There were hundreds of runners ahead of me, and some were so high and far away that they looked like ants. I began to get seriously concerned. What if they all went off and left me? The pain got worse. What if I quit there and then? Only Fred riding a team of mountain goats would be able to find my wasted and totally matronly body stuck on the craggy mountainside. I still had six miles to go, and I wasn't even up the first hill! I resorted to an all-fours stance . . . wart hog in heat, I insulted myself. I attacked the steep, pebble-covered path with a vicious and renewed determination. I heaved, I cursed, I made deals with my legs: "If y'all will just make it to the top of this hill, I swear on every pair of control-top pantyhose I ever owned, I will never comment on the fact that you touch at the top"; "I will banish the phrase 'varicose veins' from my vocabulary forever"; "And may I be dipped and rolled in Nair from my head to my toes if I *ever* turn around and look at the backs of you gorgeous gams in a mirror and say *anything* that sounds like 'cottage cheese.'" By the time I finished the "leg oath," a wondrous sight appeared above me. There, only another twenty yards ahead, was blue sky! Oh, for a glimpse of something other than the dusty trail and the rectal eclipse of the sun that Fatty, who'd had the nerve to pass me, was offering as he continued to progress up the cliff ahead of me.

I made it! I had never stopped in a race before to catch my breath, but I did then. Throngs of runners began to swarm around me, so once again I was caught up in the rush. We were then running along the top of a flat, rocky ledge, and it was a good spot to relax a bit. Rule No. 1: When running cross-country, never relax to such an extent that you take your eyes off the ground for even a second. I blinked a little too long and blap, down on one knee. As luck had it, Fatty was right behind me, and he nearly decapitated me with the crotch of his Bermuda shorts as he passed over my head in an ungraceful, low-flying leap . . . what a way to go. I regained my balance and started off again. I was just starting to get a rhythm going when a steep downhill appeared. It did not seem to be such a sharp grade until midway, when I found myself almost having to sit down to keep from barreling head over heels. I thought my toes were going to pop out of the ends of my shoes while my thighs acted as air brakes. Several other runners were falling and sliding, and I only hoped I could avoid a belly-buster on the path. Again, we reached a flat surface, but it too disappeared around a bend, and suddenly, I was staring straight up a grass-covered hill that seemed to be never-ending.

I began a pitiful climb up the hill, and as other runners passed me, I weakly reached out as if begging for alms. It was impossible for anyone to run, but the sickening thing to me was that people were smiling as they walked . . . and they walked fast! I thought all people walked the same. Maybe only matrons do. I didn't care anymore. I wanted to quit. Boston was a cakewalk in comparison. A sort of fatigue overtook me and resulted in delirium. I mumbled something about being left to the Indians. My God, I thought, Colter must have been some kind of spry guy.

I was at the top. I don't know how I got there, but luckily a very scenic and gently rolling path emerged over the next two miles. My faith started to return, and word began to filter back that we were approaching the river, which meant the finish was near. I had a lot in common with horses who sense the barn is in sight . . . my stride picked up. I saw the river in the distance and was ecstatic. I ran down the last hill and began the final approach, but something wasn't right. I got closer and closer to the water and saw that a ski rope was stretched from one side of the river to the other . . . about 120 feet across. I slowed down as I watched runners in front of me enter the freezing water of the Gallatin, and they were not knee deep . . . they were chest deep! A man in a wetsuit stood in the middle of the river holding onto the rope and assisting any runners that were accidentally swept downstream. Lots of other volunteers stood on both banks to make sure people got in and out of the water safely. I jumped in and immediately began to float downstream. I got rope burns from gripping the ski rope so tightly. I heard someone screaming on the far bank, "Hang on, Kathy, you've almost made it!" It was Fred, and he was helping people climb out of the river. Seeing his face invigorated me just enough to half swim, half hop through the rest of the swirling water. He reached out his hand to pull me out and frowned. "Nice underwear, honey," he whispered.

I looked down at my dripping shorts and gasped! I had worn my red Coca-Cola underpants with the different colored bottle tops all over them, and they were showing through my white, soaking wet shorts. I was ready for it all to end, but I still had two hundred yards to go inside the park. I huffed and puffed, and I seemed to get heavier and heavier due to the mud hanging on my feet and ankles. I heard someone coming up behind me, and glancing a bit to the side, I saw that it was my "Moon over Montana" pal, Fatty, in all his corpulent splendor. After all the misery I had put myself through, he was not going to beat me! I turned on what little speed I had left and barely finished before him. However, Fred, king of erotica, who had gone to the finish line to check out my underwear at closer range, declared it a photo finish.

As I sat drinking coffee, wrapped in a newspaper diaper Fred had fashioned while he went to find me a towel, I reflected on my performance. Where had I gone wrong? I decided I had underestimated the course and overestimated my conditioning. I was getting chilly since the wind was picking up, so I gathered my newspaper to walk to the car and hopefully run into Fred and a towel. I was nearly mowed down by a pickup truck with someone waving and yelling out of the back. There was Fatty stretched out in a lawn chair in the back of the truck, guzzling beer and hollering to anyone he came across. "Hey, good race, lady, see ya next year," he said as he tipped his cap in my direction. Then he added, "Oh yeah, thank your pop for helping to pull me out of the crik!" and he chuckled so that his chin bounced up and down on his chest.

"My pop?" I thought. "He thought Fred was my father?" I reached the car and found Fred digging a towel out of the trunk.

"Feeling OK?" he asked. "Are your legs stiff?"

"Stiff . . . these legs? I never felt better in my life, Dad," and I gave him a heartfelt kiss right on the top of his shiny head.

Kathy Schmook

CHAPTER VI

Take A Hike, Ike

I DECIDED TO take a temporary rest from running, so I accepted an invitation to hike through the hills with my friend Beulah. I liked the idea of a scaled-back activity, and I naturally assumed that I was surely in shape for any challenge hiking might offer. I quickly learned that running and climbing use two totally different sets of muscles. In fact, my first hike with Beulah was the second most painful experience of my life . . . the first one being the day after the memorable John Colter Run.

We set off early one cool August morning, and she said we'd just walk the hills a bit. I had dressed in a pair of memsahib shorts. Which my Banana Republic catalogue promised were adequate for strolling in a genteel fashion or riding a bejeweled elephant. I also wore a tank top with a light wool shirt over it since Beulah said the temperature could change drastically in the mountains at times. My "If it's not in *Seventeen*, I don't wear it" daughter appeared as I was leaving and critiqued my hiking attire, "What's the story on the knee socks, Mom?"

"These were on page forty-two of the catalogue along with the shorts. What do you think?" I foolishly asked Lisa, who lacked even the slightest tact.

"Well, like, what's wrong with your knees?" she asked.

"My knees? What are you talking about? Nothing is wrong with 'em."

"It's all wrinkly around them . . . kinda like they're smiling," she specified.

At that moment, Bruce walked in the kitchen for his early morning eye-opener of Tang, Ovaltine, and Kool-Aid and put in his two cents, "Yeah, Mom, it's like somebody hung their lassos on your knees."

"Can't y'all ever say anything nice to me? Mothers need compliments, too, sometimes. Besides, there's nothing I can do about the pull of gravity as it takes its toll on the human body." Then I stormed out of the kitchen.

"I'm just kidding, Mom," Lisa shouted, "I hope I look just like you when I'm your age."

To which Bruce gurgled with a mouth full of his plastic drink, "I hope you do, too, fatty, then I can call you "Lasso Legs."

I slammed the front door as the inevitable fist fight began.

Beulah started me off with an easy walk along the base of a group of hills that surround a mountain known as Emigrant Peak. We had taken a Western wildflower and bird book along, and I listened attentively as Beulah, who had grown up in the area, pointed out bluebirds, meadowlarks, shooting stars, and wild lupine. As the sun began to move overhead, we began our ascent of the hills; however, let me emphasize that Beulah's idea of hills and my idea of hills were two different things. North Georgia had hills. The things I was panting and straining muscles all over were full-fledged mountains to me. Beulah never appeared even to breathe hard, but not only did I sound like a buffalo with emphysema, but I was also soaking wet with sweat. I began to peel off clothes and stuff them in my "fanny pack," and by the time we reached our destination, which was the top of a hill (so-called) sprinkled with pine trees and fragrant sagebrush, I was down to my memsahib shorts, my tank top, and my Hilton Head Island visor. The socks had been the first to go since I caught them on innumerable twigs and raspberry bushes, and they continually rolled down to my ankles. As I crumpled in a heap to rest from the hike up, I drank every bit of water in the canteen I had brought along. Beulah recommended that I save some for the walk down, but I did not heed her advice . . . I figured I'd get a refill out of one of the creeks we had passed on the way. I stretched out in the sun and focused my eyes on Emigrant Peak as it loomed above us. I commented to Beulah on how beautiful it was with bits of snow still clinging to it in places. She said she and some of her friends climbed it every year . . . it rose over eleven thousand feet, and its majestic face was the aesthetic focal point of the valley. She commented that she would be sure to let me know when they climbed it during the summer and that I might like to join the group. I smiled appreciatively and made a mental note to come down with an instant case of acrophobia when she called with that invitation.

After an hour of rest, which left me stiff as a Popsicle stick, Beulah and I began the trek home. I wished my shorts would produce an elephant for me to ride down the hills. As I begrudgingly left our rest site, I gave Emigrant Peak one more careful look. Something about the regal mountain seemed to beckon climbers, and the more I studied it, the less ominous it appeared. I decided I would continue to admire it at home from the comfort of my Pawley's Island hammock.

The hike down was much quicker than the one up, especially since I could not seem to control my legs. They kept running away on their own. I did not know if it had something to do with my running muscles or lack thereof, but I seemed to run and stumble down the steepest parts of the "hills." As Beulah had predicted and because a llama would have had trouble keeping up with my overly zealous but accidental pace, I became exceedingly thirsty. We approached a stream at one point, but as I leaned over to slurp up a tidal wave of water, Beulah yelled, "NO!"

"What is the matter?" I asked through parched lips, nearly in a state of delirium from thirst.

"That water will make you sick . . . there are cattle in pastures above here that contaminate it."

"How sick can I get?"

"Sick enough that your horses won't be the only ones trotting around your house," Beulah said without smiling, and she shared some of her canteen with me.

We continued hiking on the steep downhill grade, Beulah carefully working her way down and me desperately trying to walk at a more controlled speed without having my knees punch themselves out of the backs of my legs. Gradually, the hills began to plane out, and the descent became more tolerable; however, my thirst had not diminished. Even though Beulah said we were on the homestretch, I was afraid my tongue would swell out of my mouth from lack of water.

Then I saw it . . . another creek at the bottom of a lush little dell. It was wide and deep, and even though it was full of lots of fallen timber, it was wet! I ran to it and once again leaned over for a gulp.

I heard Beulah come charging up behind me once again. "STOP!" she wailed. "That one will be bad, too."

Frankly, at that point I was ready for Beulah to leave for Beulahland, and I answered her with poisoned water streaming from my mouth, "Beulah, I don't care if they fought the Battle of the Little Bighorn in this creek last night. I am gonna drink this damn water!" And I did.

Beulah shook her head and said, "Well, when you're finished dumping parasites into your body, we gotta cross this stream. There's a log down here I usually use."

I followed her downstream until we came to a rotten tree that had fallen across the creek. It was fairly big around and was smooth except for the remnants of a few broken limbs protruding in places. Beulah jumped up on the end of the tree and started to walk across it with her arms outstretched. Mary Lou Retton would have envied her. She never wavered or lost her balance, and she even sped up at the end to perfect a graceful dismount. She made it look so easy. I hopped up. I hopped down. I knew from the get-go I was going in the drink.

"Come on, Kathy, you can do it," Beulah called across the creek, which was beginning to look like the Amazon.

I climbed onto the end of the log again. I took about three steps forward and hit a knob-like protrusion that was part of a broken limb. I stepped over it but immediately lost my balance. With my arms flailing, I looked like Don Quixote doing his windmill impression for Sancho Panza. A possible fall at that point on the log meant that three-inch broken limb would have entered my body in such a strategic area I'd have been plugged into the world's largest hobby horse.

I decided to sit. "I'm gonna shinny across," I yelled to Beulah, who had taken a seat on the creek bank to watch. I slowly sat down and straddled the tree. I placed both hands out in front of me, gripped the log with my legs, and began to inch my way across little by little. I felt sharp twinges of pain as nearly invisible twigs scraped the inside of my exposed thighs, but it was a lot safer than standing . . . I thought. Suddenly, the smooth wood turned wet. Beulah's hiking boots had left water on the rotten log, and it had made the surface as slick as glass. One minute I was sitting astride the slippery spot, the next thing I knew my hands and memsahib shorts lost their traction. I spun over the side, not changing position for a second. I looked exactly the same hanging on the underside of the log as I had looked on top of it. I only hoped a possum didn't happen by and decide to mount up also.

"What do I do?" I screamed into the log, hoping Beulah heard me.

"Try it that way," she suggested, and I knew then she was enjoying the spectacle.

"Ah, hell," I muttered to myself and my horizontal love post, "I've walked through cold water before," and I dropped into the icy creek and trudged through knee-deep water to the other side. Beulah applauded.

We had only a mile left to hike until we reached my truck, but in that thirty-minute period, I was forced to deal with the chill factor, since the sun had disappeared and I was wet from the memsahib shorts down, and the cuts and bruises I had acquired as I swung under the log. I still had souvenirs of my hike etched into the palms of my hands and inner thighs months later.

My truck finally appeared on the horizon, and I gave Beulah a ride back to her house. I declined the beer she offered because my hands were so sore I didn't think I could grip the can.

"Well, I enjoyed it, Kathy," she said sincerely, "and I'll call you when we decide to climb Emigrant."

"Right, that sounds great," I answered with the zeal of a sick clam.

"You'll love it," she continued as she walked up her front steps. "It's as easy as fallin' off a log."

Climb Every Mountain

The call to climb Emigrant Peak did not come until the following summer. By the time Beulah asked me if I wanted to join her climbing group, I had actually forgotten the pain of our initial hike together. I had been hiking and hunting with Fred in the meantime, so I was a little more acclimated to walking in these Montana hills. In addition, I had studied the mountain for months from my windows and from the dirt road I ran down in the evenings. It seemed to taunt me, as I watched its complexion change. Some days it was shrouded in a cloud cover; other days, the setting sun bounced brilliant rays off patches of snow on its face, and it seemed to bathe the entire mountain in a pink glow. The tallest thing I had ever climbed was the Washington Monument, and I don't think it is eleven thousand feet. I had to climb Emigrant because it was there . . . and because I wanted to see if the old gray mare was anything like she used to be. I accepted Beulah's invitation and the mountain's challenge.

There were seven in our group, and we started walking at seven-thirty in the morning. I had invested in a pair of heavy-duty hiking boots and decided on long, baggy khakis since Beulah had stressed flexible pants to climb in. I carried my water in a wineskin slung over one shoulder and packed my lunch in the ubiquitous fanny pack. Fred said I looked like I was going in search of the clan of the cave bear. I also followed Beulah's advice on carrying sunscreen, an extra pair of socks, and bug repellent.

"What do I need the bug repellent for?" I asked her.

Beulah explained there were all types of insects that attacked at different places throughout the climb, and she added that the ticks were bad that time of year, too.

"They make me sick," I said. "Isn't there a bracelet or necklace or something like they make for dogs?"

Beulah smiled and said, "No, but believe me, Fred will take care of your tick problems. All the men out here do. They love for their wives to go hiking because they have an excuse to conduct a thorough body search." Sounded good to me.

The sun was warm by eight-thirty, and by eleven I was roasting. I started to smear on the sunscreen, hoping to cut down on the parchment factor connected with the dry skin on my arms and hands. I had seen an ad on television that said if you could write the word *dry* on the top of your hand, your skin needed a lube job. They could hold a re-signing of the Declaration of Independence right on my body. The disadvantage of using sunscreen while exercising strenuously, however, is that it clogs the pores, making sweating more difficult and thereby increasing body temperature. I felt like I was climbing in Saran Wrap from there on.

We walked for about three hours before I had the nerve to ask when we were going to have lunch. Beulah said we were eating at the halfway point, which was on top of the huge boulder she pointed to. It didn't *seem* to be that much farther, but every time I thought we were getting closer, the rock seemed to walk the other way. We were forced to move slowly because the walk was turning into an official climb, and the grassy, open meadow we were in took a dramatic turn upwards. It took two more hours to get to the appointed lunch site, and by then I didn't know whether I was going the rest of the way up. My legs had gone on strike and did not want to bend at the knee, and I knew it would be exceedingly difficult to finish the climb with the SS goosestep.

After I chowed down on a lunch of peanuts, orange slices, and water, I lay down on the rock and fell sound asleep. I must have slept soundly because I was awakened by some little black bugs having a rodeo on the outside of my open mouth. As Beulah gathered us together to begin again, I looked up to the top of the peak. It didn't seem that much farther, so I decided to continue. I later realized that the steep grade distorted the perception of distance.

We started the most difficult part of the climb from that point on. There was an area of burned timber where we had to pass through many fallen trees. It was agony having to lift the heavy hiking boots attached to my unbendable legs to step over the logs. The mountain had gotten so steep that to pick a knee up was almost to place it on your chest. The only redeeming feature of the wooded area was that it was filled with vivid red Indian paintbrush. I knew we were pretty high up because the plant is more orange at lower altitudes. Another indication that we were getting higher was that I could not stop yawning. Sometimes I had to lean on trees and yawn until my eyes watered. Beulah said it was the altitude, and she also said the air was much thinner on the top. I never knew if that meant I was not going to be able to breathe and was going to need oxygen, or that my ears were going to pop, or both. Frankly, thin air meant nothing to me since I failed every physical science course I ever took. That wasn't girl stuff.

The true test of endurance came as we began to climb above the timberline. No more grass or trees. I turned to take a look at what we had climbed so far and gasped at our altitude. Not only did I have a panoramic view of the entire valley and even my barn far below, but at just that moment a small airplane pulling an advertisement flew *below* us. I figured we had to be near the eleven-thousand-foot mark. From that point on, the only thing we had to climb on was shale rocks, which were skinny rocks that slid under your feet and offered absolutely no traction. It was like walking up a mountain of sand . . . one step forward, three backwards.

Then I was on all fours as the mountain got even steeper. Hands greasy with sunscreen were not much help. I tried to take my mind off the aching in my thighs by concentrating on the delicate little alpine wildflowers that miraculously grew between some of the rocks. They grew very close to the ground and were brilliant in color due to the cooler climate near the top of the mountain. Once I was face to face with a cobalt blue forget-me-not, but I almost sucked it off its roots when I let go with a ferocious thin-air yawn.

I brought up the rear as we approached the last leg of the climb. It was single file up to the actual apex because the nebulous trail was so steep and narrow, it dropped off into snow-filled canyons on either side. I dared not look to the sides. I kept my eyes ahead on the rocks I pulled myself up on one at a time. My companions reached the rocky perch that was the absolute zenith, and as I stepped on the last rock before I reached out and grabbed their hands, the most horrifying thing that can happen in mountaineering occurred. I heard a distant rumble, and suddenly lightning flashed. Beulah yelled, "Hurry!"

How am I supposed to hurry, I wondered, and I took a couple more faltering steps as the lightning zig-zagged through the sky in front of me. I did not believe it. I had ignored the weather once we left the timberline, so I hadn't noticed that clouds were forming. Thunder softly rolled again, seconds later the lightning ripped through the sky.

"Get off the damn peak," Beulah hollered again, "and, for God's sake, hurry!"

Oh, right, I thought, no one wants to get off this launch site to the Big Dipper more than me, but how? I was still facing up, the footing was treacherous at best, and a fall to either side meant they'd have to vacuum up the remains.

I slowly knelt down and turned to start down. CR-A-A-CK! The lightning blazed again, and I tried to speed up. But my every step sent hundreds of the shale rocks rolling down the sides of the rocky path. My ankles were turning and rolling around among the rocks. It was impossible to run. As another bolt of lightning illuminated the sky, Beulah carefully slid past me, holding the sides of her head, and said, "Did you feel that charge go through your hair?" I had. It felt like someone was tapping out an electric version of the Morse code in my head . . . the fillings in my teeth had even buzzed!

Everyone was silent as we each tried to keep our footing and descend as quickly as possible. The sky around us had turned an ominous black, and a flashlight would have been welcome. The disconcerting thing was that when I looked far below us at the valley, the sun was sparkling on the surface of the Yellowstone River. I remembered Fred telling me once that the mountains created their own weather patterns, and I also remembered hearing that lightning struck the tallest thing around . . . that meant me, since I was once again the last in line on the descent. I squatted and tried to walk. I remembered that metal attracted lightning, too. My Speidel Twist-o-Flex watch. I ripped it off and crammed it in my pocket. I tried to inch down faster on my back like an upside-down snake, but the rocks cut my hands. It began to hail, and again I felt buzzing in my head as the lightning appeared all around. "Please, God, I don't mind dying, I really don't. Just don't barbecue me!" I prayed, and I stumbled and rolled down the side of the trail into a shallow hole, surrounded by large boulders. I sat there for a minute and realized I was semi-protected from the hail because I was able to duck under one of the boulders, which formed an over-hang of sorts. I doubted that you could hide from lightning, though. Like love, the Columbia Record Club, and the IRS.

I stayed under the boulders until the hail and lightning stopped, about ten minutes more. My companions were somewhere in front of me, but I could not see them. I began to fear being left alone more than being nearly "chicken fried." What really bothered me the most was that if I never made it off the mountain, Beulah would be able to write one of those heart-rending adventure stories for *Reader's Digest* and probably win five hundred dollars at my expense!

I cautiously began my descent again and saw my group far below me, congregated at the large rock where we had eaten lunch. It did me no good to try to accelerate my pace because my ankles had given out. They had been so twisted, torn and pulled during my electronic flight from the peak that even my high-topped boots offered no support. When I finally got off the sliding rocks and hit grass again, I put on the extra pair of socks I had brought and walked the rest of the way down in my stocking feet to join my companions.

Then we were down. Ten hours after our misery began, our starting point reappeared. I was perplexed because I had not felt the thrill of victory. I was simply relieved that I still had some ankles attached to my feet, even though they were like rubber bands. At least I had not been turned into a crispy critter.

Beulah drove me home and gave me a thumbs-up as Fred met us in the driveway and rolled me out of her car. I gave her a finger, too, but it wasn't my thumb.

"How was it? I kept looking up there with the spotting scope all day to see if I could see you guys, but I never saw any activity. Did you get to the top?" Fred asked with an irritating enthusiasm.

"Did I get to the top? Does the term human lightning rod mean anything to you? Of course I did, and, I might add, I almost didn't make it off the top. Didn't you see that storm that hit about three o'clock?" I asked, exasperated and desperate for sympathy.

"No, we didn't have a storm here," he said.

"Nothing? You didn't even hear thunder or see little lightning flashes?" I asked.

Fred scratched his head and said, "Well, there might have been a little cloud or two that floated near the top, but the only thing I noticed was that airplane pulling the sign."

"I saw that plane! In fact, I was *higher* than that plane. What did the sign say?"

"Oh, just the usual: **REPENT! THE LORD'S VENGEANCE IS NIGH!**" he said matter-of-factly. "What's wrong with you anyway?"

In a barely audible tone, I answered, "Well, that explains it. I think I just experienced a preview of some of that vengeance. Must have been some trouble with the PTL Club again."

Fred put his arm around me and helped me inside. "What you need is a good rub down — then I'll get to looking for ticks."

CHAPTER VII

Don't Let Your Babies Grow Up To Be Cowgirls

I LOOKED FORWARD to owning my own horse when I moved out West because I had ridden most of my life. However, from the onset, I have had problems trying to outwit the simple creatures.

My first memory of mounting up was at my six-year birthday party, and it began a history of equine disasters. It was very trendy to have pony parties for your children in those days, and my parents decided I would have my party with my cousin, Monroe. He and I fought constantly. All he wanted to do was play doctor, and all I wanted to do was tie a rope around his waist and play horse. Neither of us wanted to party together.

We held the event in my grandmother's back yard. She had plenty of room to accommodate twenty ponies and about fifty screaming guests, and she was also out of town. I was dressed in pink organdy with a white pinafore and lots of stiff petticoats. Not a great riding outfit but a real eye-catcher while the wearer's in the saddle. I climbed on a little gray pony named Smokey and began my walk around the yard. The path went along the zinnia and marigold garden, past the hydrangea-lined stone wall, and through an arch of sweet-heart roses climbing on a trellis. After walking around once, I decided to pick up the pace and trot around the yard. Unbeknownst to me, my adversary, Monroe, was hiding behind the rose trellis. When I came through, he swatted Smokey on the behind with a rose branch full of thorns. The pony was small but swift, and he took off at a gallop — past the churn full of homemade ice cream, past the chuck wagon filled with the birthday lunch, and past the horrified chaperones, including my mother, who was pregnant, enormous, and holding her stomach. Smokey did not stop until he reached the bus stop at Club Drive and Peachtree Street and only then because I fell off and his back feet tripped over my black patent leather Sunday School shoes.

I did not ride again until I was about ten years old, when my dad bought my sisters and me our very own white Shetland pony. We named him Trigger, and we kept him in our back yard. We rode him all over the neighborhood, but our favorite race track was the Capital City Country Club golf course. The greenskeeper called my dad at least once a week to tell him the members were complaining about manure on the fairways. The ax finally fell when President Eisenhower came to play at the club on his way to Augusta for the Masters. My sisters and I had carefully filled six of the holes on the greens with manure to get even with the greenskeeper for continuing to tattle on us. That night the chairman of the board of directors called and told my dad what had happened. Luckily, the Secret Service cleaned out the cups before the President reached each hole, but the chairman threatened the law. Even though we denied it vehemently, Dad did not waver in his decision to move Trig to our farm fifty miles away.

One day my parents decided it was time to buy me my own horse. I overheard them talking and knew it was merely a clever ploy to keep me from being boy crazy, but I was thrilled nonetheless. His name was Blackjack, and from the moment I first climbed on him, that horse did nothing but try to remove me—I don't even know why he was a horse if he wasn't interested in riders. But I adored him. I vividly remember the day we bought him.

Dad and I drove way out in the country to look at a horse advertised as sleek, black, showy, and green broke. Neither Dad nor I knew what green had to do with anything, but off we went to try out what I was sure would be one of the stallions Walter Farley wrote about. We arrived at the farm, and the farmer took us out to a large pasture with a bright red barn at one end. As we entered the barn, I heard heavy breathing that reminded me of my grandfather's snoring after a few belts of his Easy Times bourbon. That should have been a clue. The farmer reached in and brought out a dancing black horse by a bridle with silver conchos on it. The horse was beautiful, just like the ones on my calendars.

"Wanna ride Blackjack, little lady?" the farmer said, smiling.

"Are you sure he's gentle?" my dad asked as we stared up the horse's flared red nostrils.

"Gentle as a lamb—I'd put my own kids on 'im if I had any," the farmer said in typical horse trader jargon.

That was all it took. I put my foot in the stirrup, hoisted myself up, and the farmer led me out to the pasture. It was lucky the farmer let go of Blackjack when he did, or he would have plowed his entire back forty with his feet because we were off at an alarming rate of speed. We sped down one side of the pasture, he jumped a hedge of low-growing poke salit, then he raced down the other side. I pulled at the reins, but they were a mere figment of my imagination. There were none in my hands. Tears streamed down my face from fear and the wind velocity. The G-force pasted a smeared smile on my face. As we approached the barn, I barely made out the "See Rock City" sign on the roof. I wondered if that's where I was going to land, after a pass over Ruby Falls, when Blackjack threw me, which was inevitable. With absolutely no break in speed, he flew past Dad and the farmer, into the barn, out the other side, then stopped. I kept going. The thing that hurt worst was the pommel (the big bump on a Western saddle)—it was sort of like a girl having a wreck on a boy's bicycle. I landed in some mud and remember seeing polka dots for a minute. My dad and the farmer ran over to me, and my dad was yelling, "Are you all right, honey? I oughta kill that S.O.B.!"

"I'm OK," I mumbled, as I spit dirt through my teeth.

"Ain't he a mover?" the farmer said, grinning with all five teeth exposed. "Jest like a race horse—fact his mama was one. Ran in lotsa races. You rode him good, too. I kin tell he likes you. He needs a little more trainin', and you'll have you a show horse!"

By then the horse was grazing calmly and glancing at me as he chewed. "Dad, I think we ought to get him," I said. "I'll ride him in our ring at the farm every day, and he'll calm down."

He never did. I can safely say that he ran away with me inside the ring and out for the next twelve years. But I learned a valuable lesson . . . never buy a horse that breathes heavier than Grandpa standing still and never trust anyone trying to sell a horse.

On Buying Ocean-Front Property in Montana

I inherited a very old horse and pony when we purchased our new home in Montana. After a few weeks I decided they were fine for the kids, but I was ready for my own horse. I wanted one that would come when I whistled and let only me ride it. One that would fight snakes and wild beasts to defend its beloved owner. One who let me ride bareback through the hills with its silken mane and tail flowing, like Flicka and Fury did. So my husband, who hates horses and thinks they should be included on an elk tag during hunting season, agreed to help me look. That was easier said than done. I was in cowboy country and could not find a horse to buy. One problem was my Southern accent. A horse trader would hear me speak and immediately he'd jack up the price of his horse three hundred dollars. I think they probably referred to that as the "redneck contingency" behind my back. They automatically assumed I didn't know the difference between a mule and a piece of fried chicken (chicken smells better). I must admit, however, they had some unique sales techniques.

We went to visit a man who advertised he had a buckskin horse . . . CHEAP . . . DISTRESS SALE. Sure enough, the horse was pretty, and cheap. I got on him and rode him around a pasture. I thought I detected a slight limp, and by the time I had loped Buck in a couple of circles, I dismounted, and he went down on his two front knees.

"My gosh," I said, "he must be lame. I've never seen a horse do that before."

"Lady," the horse trader/reincarnated used car salesman said, "are you a Christian woman?"

"Well, yes, I'd like to think so. What has that got to do with that lame horse?" I asked, rather perplexed.

"I knew it, by golly, I knew it, and so did Buck. He's down and praying . . . yessiree, praying that you'll buy him."

At that point my husband suggested that if Buck could also sing even the first verse of "I'm Just a Jesus Cowboy Out Roundin' Up My Strays," we'd take him. He couldn't.

One evening a neighboring rancher called and said he had heard I was looking for a horse. He told me he had *the* horse. It was so broke it was push-button, and it was a real looker. The next day my husband and I went to try out the horse. When we arrived, the ex-bronc rider turned outfitter/horse-trader said, "You're gonna love this horse . . . his name is R.C., and he's so gentle I can ride him with baling twine. Why, I'd put my four-year-old on him." They always mention a kid at some point during the sale.

Sure enough, the horse was beautiful, a black-and-white paint. As I got ready to get on him, I checked his breathing . . . not too heavy, no red nostrils. Only his eyes looked a little strange.

"Why does so much of the white part of his eye show?" I asked.

"Oh, he's a very intelligent Indian pony. In fact, he's off the reservation. He belonged to the chief up in Browning, Bill Running Coyote. That's why I call him R.C. I tell ya, this horse is always thinkin'."

I mounted up and headed off down the primrose path, as it were. R.C. liked to walk sideways, like a crab. One white eye was on the road and the other was on me. A Sweetheart bread truck drove by and the horse jumped into a ditch. I stayed on. The wind picked up, and a tree branch snapped in front of us. R.C. jumped, turned in a circle and began to snort. I still stayed on. Unfortunately, at just that moment, four teenage boys came by on the gravel road in four-wheelers. My entire life flashed before me as R.C. let out a loud whinny and stood up on his two back legs as if he were auditioning for the chorus line with the Royal Lippizan Stallions. He stayed up there a long time. I did not. I preferred an emergency dismount as opposed to the "get thrown and trampled" psychology, so I jumped clear.

My husband and R.C.'s owner ran down the road towards me. "Why, I've never seen that horse do anything like that since I've had him. I'm plumb shocked!" said the rancher, as we watched R.C. continue to run down the road. To which my husband replied, "How long have you had him?"

"A week!" replied the man vehemently.

We left with me rubbing gravel off my elbows and my husband muttering, "I hope his four-year-old kid can ride like Larry Mahan."

"Yeah, and I know what R.C. stands for, too . . . Running Crab."

The Auction

After many unsuccessful hours looking at many horses, some friends suggested we try an auction. I had never been to a livestock auction, but it sounded like a good place to see a lot of horses in a day. My husband said it was the last time he was looking for a horse with me, but he agreed to accompany me to the sale.

We arrived about thirty minutes after the sale had begun, and as we entered the large metal shed, we were handed a card with a number on it and were directed towards an open bar. My husband, "Don't mind if I do" Fred, ordered Scotch and asked me for my order. I didn't see any beer or wine, so I ordered what the slick-looking cowboy next to me did . . . bourbon and branch, hoping that branch was water. I thought back to the last time I drank bourbon and water . . . six of them, in fact. It happened in the basement of the Deke House at the University of North Carolina . . . right before the Duke-Carolina game. In spite of the fact I had on my new McMullen sweater and matching Pappagallo shoes, I passed out on the padded benches in the party room and missed the game. My date told me later that my mouth was open and I drooled a lot while I slept. I swore not ever to drink bourbon again. Somehow, twenty years later it seemed apropos to have one with the rest of the guys . . . and in memory of my grandfather, Easy Times Taulman.

Girded by a paper cup filled with what looked like iced tea, I headed for the bleachers while Fred went to find a program. In the middle of the arena a man led out a large red horse with no saddle and bridle. The auctioneer said, "Here's a real strong champion . . . let's start the bidding at seventy-five dollars." When the bidding was over, the horse sold for two hundred dollars. I couldn't believe it.

How cheap! The sale continued, and none of the horses was selling for over four hundred dollars. I caught the fever and began to congratulate people around me. Finally, a magnificent bay with four white stockings came out. The auctioneer said his son had run in the Kentucky Derby. The bidding started at one hundred dollars. I couldn't help myself, I said one-fifty. Then it went to two hundred. I stuck my card up and it was two-fifty. A fat lady wearing the world's largest Sansabelt blue jeans battled me to the end. I all but swooned as I bought the horse for five hundred dollars. I quickly regained my composure and floated down through the stands. I wondered why no one was shaking my hand to congratulate me on my financial wizardry. As I walked around the sales arena, I bumped into Fred, who was carrying two more drinks and a program. Before I could tell him the good news, he said, "Hey, did you hear someone just bought the stud service of that big bay whose colt was in the Derby?"

"It was me!" I screamed in jubilation. "Can you believe how cheap he was? I got him for only five hundred dollars!"

"What do you mean? We don't even have a mare!" Fred's face was turning red, and the place where there used to be hair had a vein pulsating near the skin surface.

"So what, he and Sam will be good friends—boy, these Montanans sure don't know their horses," I said somewhat smugly.

I noticed a glazed look had come over Fred's face as he explained, "Kathy, you just paid five hundred dollars for a stud fee . . . that means you paid for breeding, get it? You have nothing tangible to show for your money!" He then drank both drinks as we went to find the owner of my prospective stud. The owner was very understanding, and we were able to sell our service behind the scenes to the fat lady in the Sansabelt jeans. I made Fred lie and say that I was suffering muscle spasms, caused by a fall from a horse, that caused my hand to jump away from me at times . . . like during the bidding. I should have known better. I had fallen victim to studs before.

Annabel

Someone finally gave me a horse. My husband's lovely aunt was visiting from Idaho and heard me lamenting over not having a horse of my own. She and her husband bred thoroughbred race horses, and they had one that could not race due to a tendon problem. She offered to send the two-year-old filly over if I wanted her.

I waited anxiously for the horse to arrive. When she did, I all but gasped as she stepped from the trailer. She was a stunning bay and huge. She had a wonderful disposition, and in the spring I gave her to a trainer to break.

The first time I got on her was wonderful; I never wanted to get off. We spent many hours riding in the mountains, and I tried to teach her not to be afraid of the streams and the jack rabbits or the deer. She did pretty well until the day a young fawn jumped up about twelve inches from her front foot. The fawn ran one way, and Annabel went the other . . . right under a low branch, which sadly enough caught me right about lip level. I didn't lose any teeth, but my lips looked like a couple of snail shells clamped together for awhile.

In fact, one of Annabel's disadvantages was her height. I have been nearly decapitated by our clothesline, our barn door, countless trees, and once she even deposited me on the overhanging roof at the Old Saloon. That time I had an audience, so I pretended that I meant to come off. My husband built a little wooden stool for me to use to mount up, but if no one was looking, I usually just stood on the hood of his pickup and swung on.

The only other problem I had with Annabel was her feet. She did not like being shod, and she seemed to know instinctively when the blacksmith was coming. I'd go to catch her, and off she'd go. Tail up, ears forward, she would gallop to the far side of her pasture. I'd sneak up to her holding some grain, and she'd wait until I was just slipping a rope around her neck, then toss her head and trot away. I tried many blacksmiths, but she hated them all. I decided she just didn't like men. One day I suggested that to a special thoroughbred farrier who was my last hope. I asked him if he would mind wearing a dress and removing his hat to put the shoes on. He refused, and even though he caught Annabel, she kicked him . . . right in the can (of Skoal, that is).

Well, I don't blame her, actually. I wouldn't want someone nailing hot circles of iron on my feet either. So, I have come up with a fabulous invention that will revolutionize horseshoeing. Using the same concept as the Lee Press-On Nail, I have designed the Schmook Step-On Shoe! Yes, indeedy, Velcro horseshoes! No more split hoofs, no more chipping, and no more nasty nail holes. And not only do they come in all sizes from Shetland to Percheron, but they also come in colors! I have created designer horseshoes for the more discriminating horse. I have shades of divine pastels for palominos, leopard spots for buckskins, some really hot zebra stripes for pintos and, my personal favorite, the brown suede desert boot for the executive hoof. I have created one style of Hoofpuppy for the horse that likes just to kick back now and then and take a nerd for a ride. Now when Annabel sees me bringing out a box of Schmook Step-On Shoes, she runs to see which ones she gets to wear. I'm in the process of making her some rhinestone shoes to wear in the Fourth of July parade next year. They will be an exclusive, and I shall call them my "Hot to Trot" design.

I knew my Junior League training in marketing would come in handy one day.

Kathy Schmook

CHAPTER VIII

Head 'Em Up

NEXT TO HORSES, cows are my favorites. I think they are cute. Ever since the days when Girl Scout troops from all over Georgia were invited to milk Rosebud, the cow at Mathis Dairy, I have loved their wet, rubbery noses and soft brown eyes. A lot of my neighbors have cows on their ranches. Some are dairy cows and some are raised for beef. In fact, one of my neighbors is raising some of the Slenderella beef that is lower in fat, to send back East to weight-conscious Yankees. I used to think all cows looked like Rosebud, but they don't. She was black-and-white polka-dotted and was called a Holstein. Out here we have black ones called Angus. There are also Herefords with white faces, and some people raise Charolais . . . I think they moo with a French accent.

I wanted to have some cows at my house because I felt they would add a bucolic ambiance to the yard; however, my husband, Fred the Barbarian, said if we raised cows, we had to slaughter them when they were grown. Never could I kill my rubber-nosed darlings.

In the spring, ranchers move their cows to pastures up in the mountains; then they bring them down again in the fall. I was spellbound the first time I literally ran into a modern-day cattle drive. I was out for a jog early one morning when I heard a distant mooing, followed by a lot of whistling and yelling. As I crested a hill on the narrow dirt road, I saw below about two hundred head of cattle. There was a cowboy in the front, a couple more on the sides, and others bringing up the rear. There were also three black-and-white dogs barking and nipping at the heels of the cows to keep them in line as they plodded along. As they approached, I realized I had nowhere to go since the narrow road was bordered with barbed wire.

I moved as far to the side of the road as I could manage and sucked in my stomach, hoping I wouldn't slap some unsuspecting cow with it, but it was impossible to move entirely out of the way. I found myself saying ridiculous things like, 'Scuse me"; "Could I get by, please?"; "Sorry"; and "Oh, was that your foot?"

The cowboys rode by smiling and waving, and I overheard one of them say, "I think that's Fred's new wife . . . talks like she's from someplace in Texas."

Another one said, "How do you know?"

To which his friend replied, "Heard it on the bovine," and they galloped off.

I watched as the entourage disappeared down the lane, hoping that one day I would be able to help someone move their cows. Not a week later, one of my friends called and asked if I would like to help her and her husband take their cows into the hills on the following Saturday. "You bet!" I said excitedly, and as I hung up the phone, I thought back to the way I had spent some weekends in the city.

Friday nights were sometimes devoted to a Braves baseball game, which was every bit as exciting as watching golf on television. The Georgia Tech or University of Georgia games were always fun unless they were playing each other. Then the rivalry became downright boring. Eventually, the emphasis became not who had the best team, but who had the dumbest players. And Sundays were a day for the struggling Falcons, who continually put the thrill back into the extra point. Now I had a chance to play cowgirl, and I could not wait.

I polished my boots, saddle and bridle, and I even replaced the hatband on my cowboy hat. The old one, a Christmas gift from my nubile daughter, Lisa, had "Born to Breed" written on the front. She made it in her Home Ec/Sex Education class. My husband also suggested I might need some chaps in case we rode through any heavy brush. He explained that chaps were leather pants worn over jeans like armor to protect the rider's legs.

The next day I went to the Lost Dogie Western Wear and Tack Shop. An affable young man came out of the back and said, "Howdy, little filly, I'm Biff, what can I help you with?"

I was somewhat taken aback by his salutation, but I figured it was better than being called a "big mare."

"I need some chaps to wear over my jeans, maybe something with some fringe," I replied, thinking back to Annie Oakley when she had been on television.

Biff smirked and said, "Sure hope you're gonna wear some jeans under 'em . . . gets kinda uncomfortable if you don't. Where you from anyway?"

"I live here in the valley, and I'm going to help take some cattle into the hills tomorrow," I said proudly.

"Well, then, you might like some of these 'shotguns,'" and he pulled a pair of heavy suede-looking flaps off a nail on the wall.

They weren't exactly what I had in mind, mainly because I couldn't tell which was the front or back, and they had big zippers on them. Annie never wore zippers.

"I don't know about those," I said.

"Here, let me show you how to put them on," and faster than you could say, 'Annie, Get Your Gun,' he had wrapped the flaps around, buckled them at the top in front, and zipped them all the way down each leg with an inside zipper that started at the top. I could tell Biff liked that part. I was covered in rawhide from the waist down except for a sort of circle cut out where the saddle met the rear end.

"These feel kinda loose, and they're heavy. Don't you have anything with fringe or something that shakes when you walk?" I asked in my undaunted attempt to add a little zip to my Western garb.

"Wel-l-l-l, I got one more pair of shotguns you're gonna fall in love with. Be right back," and he disappeared into the stockroom.

He returned carrying some black cowhide flaps that had red fringe going up and down the outside of the legs and red glitter running in stripes down the front.

"Forget it," I said. "That's not me. Wayne Newton maybe. Are you sure this isn't Frederick's of the West?"

"Just try 'em," he said, as he once again whipped into action, buckling and enjoying a problem with stuck zippers on the inside. "They're a little snug, just the way they oughta be—if I can just get this little bugger to zip—oh, now, here we go," and he ran his hands down the inside of both legs.

He stood back in a lather, and I looked in the mirror and asked, "You got any whips and chains to go with these?" I noticed his eyes brightened. "Just kidding. Tell you what, I'll take those plain brown ones. I'm in a hurry."

"Wanta try 'em on again?" Biff asked, breathlessly. "I could oil the zippers so they'd never stick."

"I'll take my chances," I said. I paid the Marquis de Sagebrush and left before he tried to consummate our relationship behind the cash register.

Head 'em Up, Moo'vum Out

I saddled Annabel early on "moving day" and packed us both a lunch of cheese, apples, bananas, and oatmeal cookies. I also cleverly concealed a bottle of my favorite champagne, Moet et Chandon, in one of my saddlebags to celebrate our arrival when we reached the top of the mountain.

My friend, Jan, and I rode at the back of the pack. The more experienced cowboys rode in the front and along the sides. We also had two dogs along to do all the barking and hoof-biting.

I got off to a shaky start because the first thing we did was cross a concrete bridge over the Yellowstone River. The river was moving very swiftly due to the snow melt, and it made a rushing sound as it went under the bridge. Annabel turned into a wooden horse at that point. She took one look at the foamy water and did a leg plant with her two front feet that said, "No way, Jack, I ain't goin'!" I kicked, cajoled, even whispered "Alpo" in her alert ears, but she wouldn't budge. It was apparent to me she had failed Bridge Crossing 101 in school. Finally, I had no choice but to dismount and drag her across since Jan and the cows were moving ahead without me. The dismount was not bad, but getting back on was an acrobatic feat Buffalo Bill would have envied. Not only was I faced with the usual problem of Annabel's height, but at my daughter's suggestion, I had worn her "totally awesome" Guess jeans under my "shotguns," and they were a size too small. I could lift my foot only high enough for the mere tip of my boot to graze the stirrup. In addition, now that we were across the bridge, Annabel was ready to go, so she would not be still! I pulled her over to the short extension of the bridge that was not over the water. I tried to stand on the narrow curb and climb up, but I was still too low. Where was a pickup truck when you needed one? Annabel kept pacing around in circles; I got her to stand still for a few seconds, while I was forced to stand on top of the ledge on the bridge and *leap* into the saddle. It was a fairly smooth landing, with only a minor pommel bruise, considering I leapt from the wrong side. I didn't have time to put my feet in the stirrups before Annabel was chasing the cattle. I caught up with Jan quickly, and she commended me on my innovative mount. She said I bore a striking resemblance to a prehistoric bird, the pterodactyl, with my arms out and my shotguns flapping in flight.

Once under way, I got the hang of things. My job was to watch for the strays and steer them back into the herd. Luckily, very few wandered away. One little calf got separated from his mother at a fence. When I rode around to try to direct him back through the gate, he ran right through the barbed wire. I tried to catch up with him to see if he was hurt, but by then he had found his mother, and she didn't look too friendly.

We climbed higher into the hills and rode through fields of powder blue forget-me-nots and hot pink wild geraniums. Then we passed through forests of fallen timber, sprinkled with spicy-smelling evergreen trees. The cows seemed to know right where they were going, and they seemed excited about getting there. Must have been like summer camp. Jan suggested I might want to dismount and tighten Annabel's cinch since our climb was getting steeper. I wasn't thrilled with the idea because I remembered the agony of getting back on, but I decided to get off and maybe have the banana that was in the fanny pack I'd worn around my waist. I swung my leg over Annabel's back and suddenly the entire saddle slid around and ended up on her stomach. I ended up sitting on my fanny pack about three feet away, which was lucky because Annabel did not like the new placement of her saddle. She started bucking and running, and she darted off into the herd of cows, scattering them everywhere. At one point while surrounded by frenzied cows, she got too close to one and it kicked her. It didn't really catch Annabel, but it did catch my champagne, which was flying around wildly in the saddlebags. The champagne started to spew, the final blow. Annabel jumped and twisted and snorted, and, finally, the saddle worked itself off. The whole incident transpired in about three minutes, but it took an hour to gather up all the cows. I didn't get to help do that because it took me that long to get my saddle back on and pick up the broken glass.

When we stopped for lunch, the cowboys were very sympathetic, but Jan suggested that next time

I leave my bottles at home. She had to share her lunch with me because my banana was smushed, the cheese had dirt and pine needles stuck in it, and Annabel ate both apples and the cookies.

I rode into my yard at dusk after being in the saddle for ten hours. I was numb from the neck down. The other cowboys had gone to the saloon, but I did not have the strength even to raise a hand to my lips. Fred found my trusty steed and me on the other side of the barn staring into space. He offered to help me unsaddle, but all I could do was whimper. He gently pulled me off and whispered in my ear as he did so, "How does a hot bath and cracking open that bottle of Moet et Chandon sound tonight?"

Annabel and I both looked at him and rolled our eyes.

Branding

Since my first ignominious experience with cattle, I have been on many other cattle drives, with a little more aplomb, too. Even my children enjoyed riding along at times. One Saturday morning, my son, Bruce, got a call from a friend inviting him to go to a branding.

"What's that?" I asked, as I finished my third helping of raspberry pancakes with blueberry syrup.

"You know, that's where they burn a little sign on the calves to show who they belong to," Bruce answered. "We're going to ride our horses over to McFarland's to help brand his cows," and he was out the door to saddle up his horse, Sam.

Later that morning I went for a jog and decided to run over to where the branding was being held. As I approached I heard strange noises, not moos, but more like naw-w-w-w, naw-w-w. And there was an awful smell that reminded me of the time I left my wet running socks on top of the steam radiator too long in a hotel room in New York City. Someone passing by my room called the front desk to report the possible death and decay of a pet.

I followed the direction of the noise and came upon two corrals. The larger one was filled with mother cows bellowing for their young, and the smaller one held the calves, the horses and their riders, cowboys of all ages, and something that looked like a short-legged barbecue grill.

I saw Bruce, who was sitting on the far side of the corral and practicing throwing a rope. I motioned him over.

"Hi, what's going on, and what is that terrible smell?" I asked.

"Mom, this is so cool. In a minute, I get to help wrestle some baby calves down so they can brand them. That's what the smell is. See that little grill thing with the fire in it? That's what the branding iron sits in till it's hot enough to burn the brand on. Then Bill or Hank puts the iron on the calf, and Jimmy cuts 'em. Butch is the ball boy."

"Cuts what?" I asked.

"The balls . . . on the baby bulls!" Bruce replied, as though he were talking about applying a Band-Aid. "Then Butch comes by with his bucket to pick them up. Some of them he throws on the fire, and the guys eat 'em . . . they're called Rocky Mountain Oysters."

"What's that guy doing with those giant plier things?" I asked, as a cowboy leaned over a squalling calf.

"If the little bulls have horns, they have to cut them off, too." And he ran off to take his turn at wrestling.

As I tried to digest what Bruce was telling me, I began to feel somewhat queasy. I tried to tell myself that the bulls were just undergoing a sex-change operation, and naturally it would follow that their horns would have to go, too. Probably dangerous to have a horny "it" cow walking around. I decided that's probably what happened to Boy George. I also understood why the cow jumped over the moon . . . he was at a branding!

I heard someone yell, "Look, Mom!" and there was Bruce lying on top of a squirming calf that had a rope around his neck and one around his feet. Another grown cowboy was helping Bruce hold the calf in place. That poor bull was going to get the whole treatment. They branded him, and I winced. Then someone snipped at his little horns, and I nearly fainted. But when someone castrated him and the blood spattered on Bruce's Max Headroom T-shirt, I lost it. I felt the raspberry pancakes begin their march upward, and I left the corral area desperately looking for a place to throw up.

I cannot stand to see a grown woman vomit in public, especially if she's sober. It's so degrading. I think it goes back to my childhood when those sudden viruses overtook school-aged children. I was overtaken once in fourth grade, but I knew enough to raise my hand and ask to go to the office. I never made it. They made me sit on a sofa in the hall outside the office because the nurse was busy, and I threw up lots of vegetable soup all over the floor. The worst part was that my class had to walk right by me on their way to the library, and they all saw me crying and having my face wiped by the nurse. It was inherent to hate anyone that threw up in school, and my classmates emphasized that fact as they walked by pointing and holding their noses.

The painful memory flooded back to me as I ducked behind a trailer and lost my pancakes. Unfortunately, Bruce picked the same trailer to hide behind while he and his friend Butch tried out the Skoal one of the cowboys had given them.

"Mom!" Bruce exclaimed, as he came around the corner of the trailer. "What are you doing back here on your knees?"

"I'm just looking for four-leaf clovers. What are you doing back here with that can?" I said, hoping he wouldn't notice the tell-tale shoulder raises that go along with the dry heaves.

"Jimmy gave me and Butch the last of his snoose to try. All the guys chew it!"

Frankly, at that point I didn't care if they both chewed and choked on one of those oysters, I had to get out of there.

"I've gotta go home now, boys. I'll see you later," and I hurried down the road towards home.

I learned a valuable lesson about brandings that day. Never attend one if you suffer from any of the following ailments: 1. A hangover (headache will be magnified); 2. A full stomach (you will throw up); 3. PMS (you will cry).

Two weeks later my balding yet hopelessly romantic husband surprised me with a trip to celebrate our first anniversary. He told me only that he was taking me to some sort of a fair and that we would eat when we got there. We drove for about an hour and arrived at the fairgrounds in Wilsall. I heard country music, gunfire, rodeo announcers . . . lots of fun-sounding events going on. I also smelled something vaguely familiar that I could not put my finger on. Fred told me to stay in the car while he bought me an official fair T-shirt. He came back a few minutes later with a tangerine shirt. I was aghast as I read the front of it: "WELCOME TO THE TESTICLE FESTIVAL . . . HOPE YOU HAVE A BALL!"

Don't Fence Me In

According to Robert Frost, "Good fences make good neighbors." Fine deal, Bobby, but I doubt he ever had to pull his hair, clothes or horse out of a barbed-wire fence . . . I doubt they have them in New England, although I'd bet my husband's flyrod a Yankee invented them.

The very first time I went for a jog down the dirt road near our house, I found out what a barbed-wire fence can do. All I had to do was lift a circle of wire off the end of a log pole which acted as a gate, and the fence should have collapsed, I would have stepped across it, then stood the gate back up, and slipped the wire circle back over the log's end. That did not happen. Apparently Hulk Hogan had set the wire "lock" on the gate because it was next to impossible to move it up or down. After splitting my paper-thin fingernails even more, I managed to push the wire off the log, which quickly resulted in a vicious and unforeseen attack by the gate on the leg of my sweatpants. I was utterly amazed! I had never been eaten by a fence before! The attack was endless. As I leaned over to remove the barbs from the fabric, more of them stuck. After much manipulation and cursing, I pulled the gate away from my pants and held it at arm's length as I attempted to close it. I got the bottom of the log into the low wire ring, but I did not have the strength to push the top of the log close enough to the wire to secure it. I momentarily forgot the man-eating nature of the barbs as I straddled the lowest strand of wire and embraced the undulating log, which was difficult to control since the wind had picked up to about forty knots. I tried to push the log close to the fence, but the barbs on the gate behind me grabbed the back of my sweatshirt and pants. I let go of the log, which jumped back and hit me so squarely on the chin that it knocked me to the ground. Sitting amidst and on top of barbed wire may be impressive to snake charmers or gurus, but it is agonizing to a runner in a Banana Republic jogging suit. I was basically impaled and had no choice but to shred my clothes as I frantically tried to extricate myself. I seemed to get nowhere fast and became hysterical as I imagined the headlines of the *Enquirer*: "WILD ANIMALS FEAST ON BODY OF NUDE WOMAN WHILE SADISTIC FENCE HOLDS HER CAPTIVE!"

Fortunately, a rancher carrying some hay on the back of his pickup drove slowly by and realized I needed some assistance. He gently helped me up while together we pulled the wire from my clothes, which were dotted with blood. He offered me a ride home, but I declined and asked only that he put the gate back up for me. He did so with absolutely no effort, and as he climbed in his truck, he said, "Why didn't you go 'round the bend there and walk across that dried-up crick? No gates to bother with."

I like lying down in wire on dirt . . . that's what we do down South, that's why, I thought to myself, but I simply shrugged and started walking home. My main concern was not the pain I felt, nor was it the fact I had ruined my new jogging suit. It was having to tell my husband that something with wire teeth prevented me from opening a gate. I decided to tell him it was a swarm of killer bees.

I asked my husband and some friends if they knew who invented barbed wire. I thought Klaus Barbie, the Butcher of Lyon, made sense, but they said it had been around for a hundred years. In fact, one day my husband showed me his valuable collection of antique barbed wire, including a small piece of the very first wire ever used in Montana.

He had carefully arranged and nailed all the wire on a huge board, and the finished product was a very handsome piece of abstract art. We decided to hang it in our living room over the fireplace, so I helped Fred move the massive piece from the barn to the house. As I leaned over the work table to pick up my side of the heavy board with the wire on it, the entire front of my shirt was instantly grabbed by the first barbed wire ever used in the state of Montana. A very concerned Fred said, "Hold your breath and put the board down gently so that you don't hurt the wire."

"Hurt the wire! You better hope I'm holding my breasts or there're not gonna be any when I stand up! I'm stuck, and my back is killing me! I'm gonna drop this thing!" And with that, the board started falling, taking with it the entire front of my second new jogging suit from, where else, Banana Republic.

Not only were my clothes getting torn up, but the kids were losing large clumps of hair. Seemed like every day I'd be out feeding the horses and I'd come across another tell-tale bunch of hair . . . Bruce's blond, Lisa's pink. I asked Fred if we could string another kind of wire and confessed that I failed to see the value of barbed wire at all. Why not use plain old skinny wire or chicken wire? He explained that it would be very expensive to change and that originally the barbs were needed to deter cattle from breaking through fences. I asked why plain wire with smelly stuff on it couldn't be used . . . like maybe a hunter's long underwear after a week in hunting camp. Fred said the idea was to confine livestock, not kill them.

I got used to dealing with barbed wire because I had to. It was everywhere. If it wasn't strung on a fence, it was lying around loose and dangerous, waiting to devour the leg of some poor unsuspecting animal. However, I didn't know it lived in the water, too.

One fall afternoon, Fred insisted I go fishing with him (see chapter 10). I told him it was too cold, but he said I could wear his fishing waders. Oh, joy! (Waders are giant rubber pants that come up under the armpits like science teachers' do and are held there by suspenders. They are supposed to keep avid fishermen dry while they stomp around in the water trying to catch fish in their pockets, I guess.)

We went to a creek up in the hills where Fred assured me I would catch a fish. I waded out into the shallow but rushing water, being careful not to slip on the rocks. As I slid into a deep, somewhat hidden crevice, something that felt like a vise grabbed my ankle. I hollered for Fred, but he couldn't hear me over the rush of the water. Suddenly, I lost my footing and not only were both feet in the hole, but I was sitting in it, and my pants were filling fast. I could not imagine what was holding my feet so securely. I hadn't heard of barracuda in Montana, but I didn't know for sure. I jammed my hand into the freezing cold water, and then I felt it. It was some damned barbed wire! I kicked, cussed, pulled and tugged. The heavy boots attached to the waders came flying out of the hole. Rubber was ripping and shredding in every direction. Not only was the water temperature causing me to act irrationally, but my temper also got the best of me. I was sick to death of running into barbs, and as I crawled onto a large boulder, I looked at the large ball of wire entwined around the bottom of the waders . . . waders that were no longer attached to the ones I had on. Then I saw him. His mouth was open and his eyes were bulging. It looked as though he was emitting a series of silent burps as he tried to speak, "My . . . waders . . . where are they?" he gasped, as I stood up on the boulder, and Fred looked at what then looked like rubber lederhosen.

"For your information, it was a "wahoo wire" fish that ate 'em, and I don't want to hear a word about it!" I said, ready for a fight.

In exasperation, Fred asked, "Well, while it ate them, did you also happen to feed it my fly rod?"

I had forgotten the fishing rod in my frenzy to get out of the wire, and we never saw it again.. We rode home in silence. Fred, in mourning over the demise of his waders and lost rod, and me, wondering if a roll of barbed wire could be named correspondent in a divorce trial.

CHAPTER IX

A-Hunting We Won't Go

I WANTED TO BE Fred's best friend. I wanted to be his confidant, his pal. I wanted to fit in. I wanted to become a part of what went on in the mountains of Montana, to experience life in the great outdoors to the very fullest, and that meant only one thing: I had to acquire an absolute passion for hunting wild game. There was nothing on the face of the earth that created more of a fervor in my husband (including the *Sports Illustrated* swimsuit issue) than the sport of bringing down a deer or an elk, an antelope, bear, mountain lion, moose, or, Lord help me, a buffalo. Somehow, I had to feign a zealous interest in high-powered rifles. Me, the one who thought the NRA was a retirement plan the Junior League offered. But I was determined. I did not want Fred to think he had married Little Miss Muffet, so I gave it my most enthusiastic "You bet!" when he asked me if I wanted to go hunting with him during my first fall in Montana.

I actually had held a gun before. In fact, I was quite proficient at Camp Merrie-Woode with a .22 rifle. I brought home all my targets blasted with hundreds of holes to show my grandfather. He used to give me a nickel for every bull's-eye. After he'd seen enough summer-camp target trophies, he thought I needed to learn to shoot a shotgun, so he took me skeet shooting at his farm. I never was very good at that. I never understood how I kept missing the big yellow clay disks with my giant red bullets. I didn't grasp the fact that little BBs blew out of the red-paper shells. He later got me professional help at the Cloister in Sea Island, Georgia. He took me every morning for two weeks to their skeet shooting range and a man named Mr. Missledine tried his damndest to make me concentrate on the soaring targets while I was having an awful time keeping my eyes off his virile young assistants with the Beatle haircuts.

Fred had the Herculean task of taking up where my grandfather had left off, lo those many years ago. He took me down a dirt road up in the mountains and set up a target. He handed me a gun that he called a 7-mm rifle; he explained how it worked and said that we would sight it in to be sure it was accurate. Then he showed me how to load and unload, and he handed me the bullets. They were three times the size of the .22 bullets I remembered using, and they seemed to be made of copper, brass, and lead. They looked like suppositories, from Bulgari maybe. There was a telescope-like thing that sat on the top of the rifle called a sight, and it magnified the targets so that they seemed closer. Fred then set up a little bench for me to prop the gun on to make it level. He fired a few times at first and hit the center of every target . . . most impressive. Then it was my turn. He gave me some earphones to put on to muffle the noise and handed me the gun. I aimed and tried to get the bull's-eye of the target lined up in the little crossed lines in the rifle sight. I pulled the trigger and blew apart the wooden frame that the target was mounted on. There was one small detail Fred forgot to pass on: do not rest the butt of the gun on or near the collarbone, could result in serious jolt. That gun nearly kicked a hole through my clavicle. Fred explained that I must nestle the gun into the fatty part of my shoulder and arm and relax. No problem with the fatty part, but there was no way to relax after the first bomb exploded on my shoulder. He also stressed the importance of keeping the eyes open when shooting, and he did say never to put my eye too close to the scope for fear of "scope eye." All in all, it seemed to be too much to think about. Nevertheless, I practiced the rest of the afternoon in my determined state to make Fred proud of his new hunting pal.

Fred decided to test the fruits of my labor at the turkey shoot in early September. He took the kids, me, and the 7-mm to the shoot and bought six tickets for the two-hundred-meter target. There were ten other men competing with me, and we were each given a number. A very brave, stupid, or drunk man, as the case may be, sat way out by the target, and after each person shot, he put their number by the hole in the target. I begged Fred not to make me shoot, but he insisted. I walked up to the little table, sat on the bench, and leveled the rifle. I couldn't even see the target, much less the man judging it. I was not able to keep the gun from swaying in the breeze, but Fred whispered encouraging words like "Hold your breath and squeeze gently," and "Watch the scope." "BLAM!" I had no idea if I hit the target, but at least there was no blood showing from the judge as he walked back with the results. I was too scared to look at the outcome, but Fred did, and I noticed he spoke to the judge for quite a while. He was kind, as always, when he told me I didn't hit the target.

"Well, what were you and the judge talking about so long?" I asked disappointedly.

"Oh, he just said that maybe we'd wanta wait awhile before you compete at another turkey shoot . . . sorta take it back to the drawing boards."

"But why?"

"Oh, he just felt like you got a little too far away from the target and a little too close to his chair . . . by accident, of course."

Fred took me back up the dirt road and made me practice many more hours.

Next came the lesson on game identification. I was somewhat insulted that Fred thought I did not know the difference between a deer and a buffalo, but one night in the saloon after a day in Yellowstone viewing game, I began to understand his concern.

A very loud and rather obnoxious man from somewhere like New Jersey came bursting into the saloon and insisted on buying everyone in the bar a drink. That's a dangerous thing to do in a Montana bar 'cause they count children and dogs in on that. He was celebrating his moose hunt and wanted to share his elation. He was dressed in typical Yankee splendor and could have passed for the Abercrombie and Fitch fold-out catalogue man. He described the adventure, the intrigue, and the hazards he had faced throughout the entire afternoon as he stalked his prey. He said he finally hid in high brush and slowly moved in on the moose as it ate. "Never knew what hit him," the New Jersey American continued, "I filled him full of lead before he got a chance to turn and charge me. He's out here in my truck, come take a look," and Fred and I followed the hunter outside.

As we approached the pickup Fred said to me, "Now you can see a moose up close." Then he said, "On second thought, no you won't."

There in the back of the truck were four legs sticking almost straight up in the air. They were long black knobby legs, but the feet looked funny. They had horseshoes on them. We leaned over the back of the truck as the hunter continued to babble, and we stared face-to-face with a mule. The worst part was that he *belonged* to somebody. He had a brand on one of his back legs.

Fred turned away in utter disgust and said, "Now do you see why you have to know your animals?"

"It would be a cold day in hell before I ever got Francis, the Talking Mule, confused with Bullwinkle," I said. "Apparently they don't play animal lotto in New Jersey."

After Fred was sure that I had no problem telling one animal from another, I had to decide what I wanted to hunt for. A deer was out. No way was I going to shoot a deer after *Bambi*; besides, I felt it was irreverent after becoming such good friends with the girls on my running road. Didn't want an elk because they looked too much like a deer in the face and because my ceilings weren't high enough to have a head mounted complete with antlers. Same was true with a moose; besides, anything that stupid deserved to live. Lions were too much trouble, and forget the buffalo. I'd have to get a Hertz Renta Buf to haul it away, then I'd have to move into a cathedral of some kind to hang the head . . . maybe Robert Schuller's?

I decided on a bear. I didn't know any personally, and a bearskin rug would be nice in the living room, add a sensual touch.

Fred lectured me for days on bears and their habitats. I suggested we just go into the woods and cook up some bacon . . . that should bring them to us. He nearly fainted at the thought of baiting a bear, not to mention that it was against the law. It seemed every idea I had about hunting was against the law. I did not want to spend the night in a tent, so we agreed to hunt very early in the morning and late into the evening.

I was standing on the edge of a steep, rocky mountainside at six o'clock in the morning waiting for the sun to come up. Fred told me I was not to fire any shots before dawn because that, too, was against the law.

"What would I shoot at anyway?" I asked, already exhausted from lugging my gun up the mountain. "I can't see anything but the dial on my watch, which is still illuminated. By the way, is there no chivalry in hunting? Do I have to carry this cannon the whole way by myself?"

"Of course you do, honey. You need it right in your hands in case you have to shoot."

As the sun began to peek over the top of the mountains, Fred said it was time to move. We walked along the side of the mountain, and as we went Fred pointed out signs of deer and elk.

"It's very important, Kathy, that you learn to look for the scat," he said. "That'll tell you if there has been any game in the area at all." He stopped and kicked over a mound of brown oval-shaped things on the ground that looked like the Pom-Poms I ate at the movies.

"What is that stuff?" I asked, fairly uninterested in the biology lecture.

"I told you—scat—or maybe you'd call it a dropping," he said, as we stepped over the Pom-Poms on the ground.

"Oh, sure, dropping? That's a turd if I ever saw one. Why didn't you just tell me? Whose is it anyway?" I asked.

"That is from a deer, and it is fresh . . . let's keep moving in this direction." We continued to walk on the rocky mountainside until we came to a small clearing. Suddenly, Fred put his finger to his lips and dropped to the ground, motioning for me to do the same thing. He pointed through the trees to a meadow, and there were six deer eating.

"Do you see that huge buck . . . that's the one with the antlers. See him? He's looking this way now . . . must smell us," Fred said, and he pulled his rifle off of his shoulder.

"What are you doing?" I whispered.

"I told you I had a deer tag, and that buck is a white tail. He'll make for good eating. Watch him now. See how he's breathing real hard, almost foaming at the mouth. Look at how swollen his neck is. He's in rut with all the does around."

"What rut?"

"I guess you could say he's in heat," Fred answered dispassionately.

"Don't shoot him to eat," I said. "Who could eat one of those? Besides, what about his girlfriends? You just can't!"

By the time I finished the Clarence Darrow defense of the deer, the entire little herd of does had looked in our direction, perked their little boomerang ears up, and jumped away in the opposite direction, led by Studly, Fred's lost meal.

"Oh, brother, this is gonna be a great hunt, I can tell," Fred said. "What do you think you're out here for?"

"To kill a bear," I said adamantly. "I cannot watch you kill a deer with a face like that."

"They all look the same, dammit. What d'ya want? Ya want them to wear a mask?" Fred asked exasperatedly.

"Just go on," I said, "let's just look for bears!"

"It looks like I don't have a choice," he said, and we started walking again.

We walked up and down mountainsides and through many creek bottoms with no sign of a bear. Fred said we could eat lunch and rest until later in the afternoon when the bears came out to look for dinner. That was fine with me. So far, the ecstasy of the hunt had escaped me. We dined on cheese and fruit, which I had brought in my fanny pack, and Fred produced a luscious accouterment of jerky and something called pemmican.

"What's that gross-looking stuff?" I asked as he handed me a wad of it.

"Great energy food, try it. It's just dried meat mixed with some nuts, and it has a few berries in it . . . very nutritious," Fred said.

I took a small bite, which stuck conveniently on the outside of my tooth, and said, "Yeah, honey, that's something, but I think I'll stick to the cheese." The pemmican looked like what I was sure the scat tasted like.

After a relaxing lunch and a snooze in the cool air and bright sun, Fred made us start the hunt again about four o'clock. He said we didn't have a lot of daylight left, and we had to hurry. I had already decided that cocktail hour was more appealing than the bear idea I had come up with.

We walked for a good hour down a dusty little game trail when Fred stopped abruptly and squatted down. "Look!" Fred whispered, "Do you know what this is?" He picked up a stick and poked a gooey brown pile with berries and grass in it.

"Yeah, somebody ralphed up their pemmican," I replied.

"You'd better get real serious about this hunt, 'cause this is bear," and Fred looked up at me like he had just diagnosed a case of herpes.

My gun was loaded, but he took it and made sure there was a bullet in the chamber. My interest began to pick up as we continued down the path, and I felt a chill run through me from time to time. I started seeing bears everywhere . . . up on the sides of the canyon we entered, then coming up behind me. My nerves began to get the best of me. Again Fred stopped suddenly, and he backed up, grabbed me, and pulled me to the ground. "He's just ahead of us!"

"Who?" I whisperd.

"Your bear . . . see him? He's down there digging in that grass around that stump . . . nice black one," Fred said. "We're gonna move slowly downwind to that thicket. Now follow me."

We almost waddled as we stooped low and moved over to hide behind some bushes. There was a large pine tree next to them, and Fred whispered to me that he wanted me to stand up, lean over a tree limb for support, then fire. He went on to tell me for the hundredth time where to aim, and he said he would back me up with his rifle in case I only wounded the bear.

The gun was loaded, and I shook uncontrollably as I stood to lean over the branch. I squinted and looked through the rifle scope, then saw the bear. I lined his head up between the little crossed lines and stood there for a minute. While I did, the bear changed positions and went from broadside to facing me, still digging up a storm.

"Hurry up," Fred said, "he's gonna smell us any minute."

I aimed the gun again, took a deep breath, held it, and fired! At least, I thought I did. I fired again and again and again in a frenzy!

"Where'm I hittin' him?" I asked, near hysterics. Fred did not answer. "Where the hell?" I half whispered, half screamed.

"Honey, lower your rifle," Fred said, and he handed me four bullets which he had picked up from the ground, intact. "I think what we have here is a form of premature ejaculation," and he took off his hat and wiped the sweat from his head.

"What do you mean? What happened?" I asked, totally confused.

"You forgot to pull the trigger . . . you ejected all four of the bullets without ever firing. Damnedest case of buck fever I ever saw. Move out of the way, I'll get him!"

"You can't shoot him, you don't have a tag," I said in frustration.

"I'll use yours, now move!"

"No!" I said, then broke into tears, "I can't watch this," I wept, "I tried to let you think I could share everything in your life . . . I wanted to be your pal, but I just can't shoot anything and watch it die. Plus I can't watch you shoot anything either. I can't even step on fire ants."

Fred took the gun from me, which I had pointed right at his belt buckle while I slobbered and drooled all over myself, and said, "I know you tried, and I'm glad you came out here to see what hunting is all about. But if you really want to be my pal, if you really love me and want to prove it, just don't ever come hunting with me again, okay?"

"I promise, I won't. But do I have to cook what you kill? I can't look at their faces, much less if they're bleeding," I said.

"No, sweetheart, don't worry. I'll do all the wild game cooking and cleaning."

"Do I have to eat it? One time I tasted some elk that my dad killed, and it tasted like he'd cooked his huntin' boots and sliced 'em up."

"I promise I'll cook it, and you'll never know what it is, it'll be so tasty," Fred said in a very unconvincing way. "In fact, you just leave dinner to me for awhile. I'd like to show you what some real Montana cookin' is all about. Now, let's start for home while we still have a little daylight. As long as we've decided to give Bruno a break this time, I don't want to meet him head-on in the dark."

"Right, and thanks for not being mad," I said as I slung the heavy rifle over my shoulder. "But tell me, sweetie, are you gonna be servin' up a lot of that pemmican in the future?"

CHAPTER X

Can Your Fish Do the Hula?

IN MY QUEST to have the best third marriage in the West, I gave up hunting for fishing. Therefore, I lied to my husband, fly-fishin' Fred, and told him, "Oh, yes, my beloved, I would adore to go fishing with you." I knew it wouldn't be as bad as hunting because fish don't have the endearing qualities that deer and fuzzy bears do. They also don't have a lot of blood in them, and I figured I could stand the slime. In addition, they don't blink. That's very important . . . "Never kill something that blinks" is my motto because that means the blinker is thinking about his demise and blinking over it.

I was not a novice to fishing. I had fished with my dad and uncle in the Gulf of Mexico, and even back then as a child, I was bored. I never caught one game fish; they fished for marlin, tarpon, grouper, and something called snook. I ended up with things like jellyfish, barracuda, sharks, and, worst of all, something called a skate, which had an electric shock to it. Every time I pulled something in they either had to kill it with a bat, shoot it with a gun, or cut the line. However, I rarely had a bite so I spent most of the time reading my Nancy Drew mystery books and daydreaming about meeting Annette Funicello and Spin and Marty on the *Mickey Mouse Club*. As I got older and was forced to fish with my family in the ocean, I decided there was definitely a Bermuda Triangle, especially created for the wives and children of enthusiastic deep-sea fishermen who would rather disappear than sit on the back of a Hatteras and watch one more grouper get hauled in.

The thing about fishing with that anglin' kinda guy, Fred, was that he liked to fly-fish. The only problem was that I didn't know what that meant. I assumed it meant that you baited your hook with whatever creature you caught. The creature then flew into the water along with the hook. Not so, I found out. The good thing about fly-fishing is that your bait is fake. Fred spent hours tying just the right fly (bait). According to him, the object was to reproduce insects in their various stages of development and put them in the water in order to fool some fish into chomping on the hidden hook. When I asked him why he went to so much trouble making his own flies and why he didn't dig worms in the garden, his face turned white, he gasped for breath, and the tell-tale vein on the top of his bald head began to pulsate — a sure sign that I had overstepped the boundaries of fly-fishing etiquette.

"Kathy," he began, trying to control himself, "I am what is known as a scientific angler . . . I take the time to study the hatch on top of and underneath the water. Then, after I have carefully determined which fly would be most like the insect in the hatch, I tie it and present it to the fish so that it floats through the air and lands gently on the surface of the water. I tie two kinds of flies, wet ones to emulate the insect in the larva stage and dry ones to imitate the flying insects. To dig garden hackle and put it on the end of a hook would be as bad as your wearing a pair of chaps and a Stetson to one of those Junior League meetings you used to go to."

"God forbid," I said in mock horror, "or, worse yet, wearing white shoes after Labor Day."

Fred was on a roll and continued to lecture me on the philosophy of the fly. "Let me put it this way: I am a purist. I would give myself a vasectomy with a rusty pocket knife before I'd put a worm on my hook. Do you understand now?"

"Honey, I never heard Jimmy Swaggart give a sermon any better . . . I'd send you money."

But Fred was not kidding. He kept a small section of our office reserved for his fly-tying, and he had hundreds of little plastic containers with things like dark moose body fibers, clipped caribou hair, elk leg hair, marabou feathers, grizzly hackle tips, a chunk of polar bear hair, and his most

151

prized possession, something called "jungle cock." I dared not ask what that was. He also had little tools that he used to construct the minute flies, and after he completed one of his masterpieces, he put them in a drawer with the name on the outside. Some of the names were hardly believable: Sofa Pillow, Joe's Hopper, Missoulian Spook, Wooly Worm, Cowdung, Elk-hair Humpy, and my favorite, the very sensual Marabou Muddler, made with silver chenille, marabou feathers with peacock topping, and gray clipped deer hair. Wow!

One summer afternoon, Fred told Bruce, a mercenary of the worst sort, that he would pay him a penny for every salmon fly he caught in our yard and around our house. A salmon fly is one of the most sickening bugs I have ever seen. They are huge and have very long legs. They fill the air near us every year when they hatch off the river. They are so big that one landed on a runway at the Bozeman airport, and they filled it with ten gallons of gas before they realized it was a salmon fly. Bruce made five dollars that afternoon, and Fred had enough salmon flies to fish with for days, which is exactly what he did.

After my lesson on bait, I had the thrill of learning to cast the fly rod. It wasn't like the fishing poles I had used before. With a fly rod, which "always-aimin'-to-please Freddy" had given me on my birthday, you have to whip it around above your head with this mile-long rope hanging out of it, then throw the line out on the water and hope the fly looks like a delicious bug to a fish. Fred always stressed to me that I must have a light touch so that the fly would barely skim the top of the water, the way a bug does naturally. Every one of my flies hit the water like an L-1011, and Fred said that it looked more like skipping rocks than the art of casting. I don't even know why there is a reel on those rods. I had to pull the string out with my left hand and hold it while I yanked the pole back and forth over my head. And woe be unto anything behind me. I caught myself in the back of the neck many times, not to mention Fred's hats, the antenna on his pickup, and an assortment of tree limbs. However, the most dangerous thing I ever hooked was a bird's nest. Not just any old bird's nest either. It was an eagle's nest, the pride and joy of the Yellowstone ecosystem. They are a protected species, and it is a federal offense to disturb their habitat in any way.

"Fred, help me pull this damn line out of that nest up there," I said, not understanding the severity of the problem.

"My God," Fred said as he looked up at the tree and my pole hanging from the nest, "that's an eagle's nest! We gotta get that line out of there. There might be eggs in it, and there are only sixty nesting pairs of eagles in this whole area. On top of that, you'll be arrested for disturbing the eagle's home."

"You mean if I had a really bad cold and stood under this tree and sneezed and coughed and had gas and scared the eagle off her nest by accident, I could get in trouble?" I asked incredulously.

"Faster than you could blow your nose," he said. "If you even picked up an eagle's feather from the ground and kept it or photographed and, in turn, harassed one, you'd be in real trouble."

"Well, what the hell are you standing there lecturing like the Birdman of Alcatraz for? What do we do?"

"I'm just gonna cut the line and leave it hanging. Then your casting lesson is going to continue somewhere else." He reached up and cut my pole free.

After that episode where, luckily, the eagle had not landed, my casting was thwarted somewhat. I was afraid to snap my line back and forth because I couldn't control what it might pick up behind me, but after many hours of patient instruction, Fred said I was ready for a day of fishing on the Madison River.

"How long will I have to wait?" I asked as I took my pole and creel (straw pocketbook for carrying fishing accouterments and my *People* magazine) from the car.

"That is irrelevant," Fred answered, as he led me down to a bank on the river. "You must remember one thing: the hours spent fishing will never be subtracted from a person's total life span."

"Did Kahlil Gibran say that or Jack Dennis, your fly-fishing hero?" I asked as I sat down and got ready to pull out my *People*.

"Every fisherman knows that to be the truth. Now let's stand out here in the water a bit," he said, and I followed him out into ankle-deep water.

The water wasn't very cold, so I decided to go a little deeper since I was having my usual run of bad luck. The water was just below my knees when Fred yelled over to me, "I wouldn't go much deeper if I were you. There might be a drop-off of some sort."

The last words I heard were "some sort" as I took a step forward and suddenly, only my visor and a pair of hands holding a pole were visible. I was forced to swim backwards underwater using only one arm, which was difficult because of the current. Fred finally made it over to me and helped pull me to my feet, all the while assuring me that lots of people "drop off." Needless to say, the fishing trip had lost its zip at that point, and I was ready to sit in the car and read. However, Fred persuaded me to stick it out, so I took my shoes off and fished ankle-deep for the next hour.

I swatted bugs and whirled my rod around in the air to break the boredom and was just about ready to call it a day when something bit my fly. "Fred, something's on my hook!"

"Reel it in," he cried, as he ran over to me.

I reeled and reeled and got lots of loops and knots in my line, but somehow a brown fish with orange dots on it landed at my feet. "I got him!" I yelled exuberantly. "You take him off the hook, though," I said to Fred demurely.

"Be careful," Fred warned, "don't let him flip out of the water. Boy, you've got a nice brown one."

"Brown what?" I asked.

"Trout," he answered as he worked the fly from the fish's mouth. "Well, I'll be, you caught him on that marabou muddler you like so much."

"Yeah, it looks like a hula skirt in the water . . . just goes to show even a fish can't resist the charms of a bug doing the hula."

Fred took the fish off the hook, then lowered it in the water and started moving it around like he was helping it to swim.

"What are you doing?" I asked.

"Just helpin' this guy get to swimmin' again before we let him go."

"Let him go? What for?"

"Sweetheart, the Madison is a catch-and-release river. You're not allowed to keep the fish," Fred answered in his official tone that I was beginning to hate.

"Catch and release this, Jack," and I pushed him out of the way and grabbed my fish out of the water.

"Kathy, what are you doing? Give me that fish, you're gonna hurt him!"

"Not near as bad as I'm gonna hurt you if you touch him again. Do you think I stood in this river all day with no wine coolers, no beer, not even any Perrier, nearly drowning, not to mention the sunburn on my magnolia-blossom skin, and then I finally catch a fish, and I'm puttin' it back? Get outta here!" And I stomped up to shore and dumped the semi-conscious fish in my creel.

Fred chased me, grabbed the creel, and a tug-of-war ensued.

"All right!" I finally yelled. "I'll let him go myself. You go back to your fishing." And for some stupid reason he believed me and went back to his rod.

I knew he was watching as I took the creel and fish down to the water. I put the creel down and picked up a large stick on the bank. I put it in the water and moved it around gently, talking to it the whole time, "Now, that's a boy. Work those little gills, flex that fin, come on and blow some bubbles, good boy . . . now, bye-bye, and beware of marabou muddlers in the future."

I picked up the creel, making sure the fish was hidden under my magazine, and went back to the car. Fred continued to fish the rest of the day and, subsequently, to pout since he didn't even get a bite, and I read. Finally, about seven o'clock, Fred packed up his gear and said despairingly, "Well, I guess you caught the only fish around today . . . I musta been using the wrong flies."

As we drove away from the river, I made a final pronouncement, "Fred, you gotta always remember your own advice and follow it: next time, tie up a batch to match your hatch."

He ignored me, and we drove home in silence . . . Frustrated Fred, and me, smugly holding my creel.

Kathy Schmook

CHAPTER XI

The Good Life

An Apple a Day, Then Maybe an *A?*

IT IS PROBABLY the institutions found in the rural West that have had the most effect on my children's lives and mine since we moved here over two years ago. One of the most important institutions in a rural environment is the country school. The only things I knew about such schools I had learned from *Little House on the Prairie,* and I certainly never thought one of my children would go to one. However, my son has gone to a little school in our area for a couple of years now where the enrollment of the entire school equals the number of children that used to be in one classroom at the city school he attended.

I liked the new school from that first day when I drove Bruce there. It sits in the middle of a pasture encircled by mountains. I watched as one of the teachers chose a child to ring the school bell. She picked a little Indian boy, and as he reached up to pull on the heavy rope, it lifted him from the ground while he giggled and landed, then pulled again. I took Bruce to his room, met his teacher and was surprised by the fact that the classrooms were combined. Bruce, who was a fourth grader, was in a room with the third grade as well, which was lucky since his previous teacher had indicated that he may as well have dropped out of school that year and gone to study aeronautical engineering at Cape Canaveral since all he did was draw rockets on his test papers. The kid just didn't operate well under pressure, and, unfortunately, once a child gets it in his mind that he's a dummy, he gives up and sets out to prove he really is.

Much to my amazement, Bruce started to come home from school laughing and talking about going back the next day. One day he even wanted to take his teacher an apple from one of our trees. I used to have to make his teachers entire apple pies to bribe them into not killing Bruce and not giving up the teaching profession altogether. Everything about the new school was laid-back and much slower. Even the school bus.

The bus picked Bruce up every day at the end of our driveway, and it made two runs throughout the valley to pick up all the kids. I do not know how the lady bus driver kept her sanity, and if there was

ever anyone who needed the bumper sticker "God
Is My Co-pilot," it was her. In contrast to my teenage daughter's bus, better known as the sex wagon,
the kids on Bruce's bus usually engaged in nothing
worse than spitballs, rubber band shots, and some
language that occasionally educated the driver.
Once our dog, Ug, got on the bus with Bruce. The
driver said, "Whose dog is this?"

Bruce replied proudly, "It's mine . . . his name is
Ug."

"Well, I'd let him ride with you, but he smells
too bad. Now make him get off."

Seemed that Ug had gotten into another scuffle
with a skunk the night before, and the odoriferous
aftereffects were just too much for the bus at eight-
thirty in the morning.

In the past, my conferences with Bruce's teachers
were like waiting on an audit from the IRS. I'd sit
in the hallway tearing my cuticles to shreds knowing what was coming. Things were different at my
first conference here. He "played well with others,"
he "respected school property," he "followed
instructions."

"Are you sure you're talking about the right
child?" I asked the teacher. "How about his hyper-
activity? What do you do when he gets fidgety?"

She answered very matter-of-factly, "I make him
go outside and run around the school building till
he's tired and ready to work again."

The tiny school seemed to concentrate on building the children's self-esteem. Every event was
designed to make each child feel special. One of

the biggest happenings of the year was the Christmas program, and every parent of every child in the school attended. No matter what the hard-working ranchers, carpenters, painters and mothers were busy doing, no one missed the school Christmas program. Every child had a speaking part, and some were allowed to play musical instruments. I remember waiting nervously as Bruce walked out in the choir the first year, and when he opened his mouth and sang a solo of the opening lines to "Rudolph, the Red-Nosed Reindeer" a cappella, I thought I was hearing things. I didn't know my little Rambo could even carry a tune, much less had the nerve to do it in public. Those flute lessons must have paid off after all!

I thought back to endless carpools I drove to baseball, soccer, and basketball practices when we had lived in the city, and at times I wondered if I was depriving my son of sharing team spirit or learning the competitive edge. But he had learned how to shoot, fish, ride a horse, and ski, things he could do alone, and I learned a long time ago that the happiest people on earth are the ones that are not afraid to be alone with themselves. Then one cold, blustery winter afternoon, I realized Bruce was learning something else, too.

The phone rang that Saturday morning, and my friend Lila was on the other end, "Kathy, I have a huge favor to ask you," she said.

"Sure, what is it?" I asked.

"Bill called from down in the park, and he is going to be stuck down there clearing roads for a couple of days. I've got lambs coming and just don't have enough hands to feed the ones that won't eat and watch the mothers delivering. I've never had to do this without Bill before. Would you mind coming over and just help me feed? It's not hard, and I'll show you how."

"Oh boy!" I said. "Baby sheep! Can I bring Bruce? Lisa is at a friend's and Fred is working."

"You bet, we'll put him to work too . . . I'm really desperate or I wouldn't ask," she said.

"What, Mom, what?" Bruce was hollering in the background.

"Wanna go to Lila's and help her with her sheep having babies?" I asked.

"Let's go!" he screamed, and I told Lila we'd be right over.

"Dress real warm 'cause it's bitter outside," she warned.

We put on layers of clothes and left. When we arrived at Lila's, she greeted us holding an old Pepsi bottle with a large nipple on the end.

"I can't thank you enough for coming. Bruce, you come with me. I've got a lamb that won't nurse, and you're gonna have to try to feed it."

She took us into her barn and amid a lot of ba-a-a-a-ing, she picked up a tiny lamb and shoved it at Bruce. "Here, take him and force the nipple into his mouth like this. He'll resist, but you keep try-ing. I've gotta get your mom to help me for a min-ute outside. Come out there when he finishes the bottle."

I followed her outside, and she pointed out the ewes that were getting ready to have their lambs.

She showed me one that had a lamb with her and told me to distract the mother so she could take the baby into the barn. Then the mother would follow. I held the mother's attention just long enough for Lila to pick up the lamb and hurry to the barn, with the mother following and wailing up a storm. I glanced around the enclosed corral, and my eye fell on a sheep lying in a corner half hidden by a tractor. I walked over to her and noticed that something horrible was coming out of her rear end. I didn't know what it was, but it reminded me of watching Bruce be born. For some reason the doctor and nurses thought I *wanted* to watch all the placenta and leftovers come out, too. I kept telling them I had only wanted to see the baby . . . no extras.

"Lila!" I screamed. "Come here!"

Lila came running from the barn with Bruce on her heels. "What's the matter?" she asked as we stood over the ailing ewe.

"What's wrong with this sheep? I think she has a baby stuck half in and half out," I said clinically.

Bruce quickly gave his diagnosis, "I think she went to the bathroom, Mom," and he knelt down beside the sheep to inspect closer.

"I'm not sure what the matter is, but that's not the baby. Maybe it's the afterbirth. I'll have to check," Lila said and leaned down over the sheep.

"You mean you're gonna stick your arm in her . . . her..."

"Butt," Bruce interjected.

"I've gotta see if she's already delivered or if there's still a lamb in there." She started to work her hand, then her arm up into the sheep.

Be my guest, I thought to myself as I looked away. This had not been in the job description.

Bruce moved around to the head of the sheep and held her head, gently stroking her while never taking his eyes off Lila.

"Feel anything?" Bruce asked.

"No, and that's not good. It's what I was afraid of. She's gone and had her lamb somewhere and this mess is her uterus. I know there is a way to stuff it back in and sew her up, but I don't know how." She looked over at me. "I don't suppose by some miracle you know anything about how to do that?"

"Oh right, that was my last Junior League placement, uterine clean-up committee at headquarters. Of course I don't know!"

Then Bruce asked quietly, "But where's the baby?"

"You go look for it. It may already be dead 'cause it's so cold, but if you find it, bring it in the barn. Your ma and I will be feeding."

"But what about the mother?" Bruce asked as he laid the mother sheep's head down gently.

"She'll be dead in a few minutes. There's nothing we can do for her. Go try to find her baby." Lila motioned for me to follow her to the barn.

A few minutes later we heard, "Mom, Lila! I found it!" Bruce staggered into the barn holding a tiny black-and-white speckled lamb tightly against his ski jacket. "Look how cute he is."

Lila frowned and said, "He looks awfully cold, Bruce. We need to warm him up and get him fed as quick as we can. Kathy, you stay here and just keep an eye on the lambs and make sure they're nursing all right. Bruce and I are going to the house with this one and see if we can save it."

I watched as Bruce followed Lila across the corral, still gripping the freezing lamb. He took a slight detour and went by the dying mother sheep. He knelt down and put the lamb's nose on the mother's face, and I heard him say, "I'll take good care of your baby." With a final pat on the sheep's woolly head, he hurried to the house to warm the lamb.

Lila said it was a miracle, but the little lamb lived. She and Bruce had put it in the oven and turned it on low. It didn't eat for a while, but after it warmed up, Bruce worked with it and it finally took a nipple. When it did, the little tail wagged like a dog's as it sucked slowly at first, then started to slurp hungrily. The lamb moved to our house the next day, and Bruce fed it religiously every three hours. That kid is gonna make some baby a wonderful father one day.

That night my parents made their usual weekly call to make sure we were still alive in the wilds, and I heard Bruce say, "Granny! Guess what I got to do today . . . I saved a lamb!" and I wished I could have seen my mother's face as he went through the play-by-play for her.

So it occurred to me that evening that young Bruce's penmanship may always be indecipherable and he may never remember who Ponce de Leon was, but he was becoming proud of his accomplishments in and out of school for the first time. He had learned a bittersweet lesson about the fragility of life. Besides, I was perfectly capable of teaching Bruce anything he wasn't getting in school . . . we studied well together.

"Mom? What did Magellan do again? I know he sailed somewhere."

"Yeah . . . I b'lieve he started the first America's Cup Race."

"And Vasco da Gama? Did he invent Florida?"

"Uh, yes, my sweet . . . that and spaghetti."

Yep, the kid is gonna do just fine.

The Old Saloon

Another integral part of Western culture is the bar. Life is hard in Montana, there's no doubt about it. Work is scarce, so money doesn't come easily, and the weather separates the men from the boys. The work that is available requires long hours of toil, sweat, grime, and frustration at times. So, when the day is done and it's time to relax, folks head for our local watering hole, known as The Old Saloon, which has been in existence since 1902.

The Old Saloon is not just a bar. I've been in bars in the city and when a man asked if I wanted to ride the pony, I ran for cover. Out here if someone asks you that in the saloon, they probably want you to help break a horse. I'm talking about a place where there are still horses tied up to a hitching post out front. In fact, it's a good thing horses can sleep standing up because they are often there for a quite a while. I loved the anachronism, so I tried tying my horse, Annabel, out front one time. I guess she was too young and got bored because she broke loose and ran back to our house, carrying part of the hitching post. My husband, Fred the saloon detective, realized at once that his bride had probably stopped off in a never-ending quest to find a mint julep, so he and his pickup saved me from a walk home.

But the saloon is more than a place for locals to drink and play pool. It is a place where information on possible jobs is passed around and where you find out who's back in the valley and who's not. If someone is in need of a helping hand, either physically or financially, both are taken care of at the saloon by a fund started in and sustained by funds from a glass jar at the end of the bar. There's pizza and football on Monday nights during the fall, and guitar pickin' and grinnin' on Tuesday nights. The warmth of the wood stove set in the middle of the bar acts as an oasis for weary hunters after a day of fighting the elements. For some that are forced to leave the valley due to work or family upheaval, the saloon is usually the last stop upon leaving and the first after returning. When Montanans get homesick, as most people do after leaving the area, the saloon is where they call to touch base.

One of the things I like most about life in the valley is that there are no silly rules, no formal code of ethics. For instance, if they tried to close the saloon on Election Day, somebody'd get cut.

And children are allowed in with their parents because the atmosphere is not that of a sleazy, smoke-filled barroom. It's more along the lines of a social hall. Everyone keeps an eye on everyone else's children, and even the bartender has been known to tell the kids to quit jousting with the cue sticks. The children are easily entertained by exchanging hunting and fishing stories with the adults, playing the one video machine, or using the pool table when the adults aren't. Lisa has, in fact, become quite proficient at the game. Last Christmas, when I asked her a bit suspiciously how she was able to afford the willow basket she gave me, she had to confess that she sandbagged a couple of smart-talking Florida boys and won thirty dollars playing eight-ball. Bruce later admitted to aiding and abetting by telling the young men that Lisa, secretly known as Montana Fats, didn't know a cue stick from a curling iron, and they willingly fell victim to the carefully rehearsed ploy.

Every Christmas the saloon organizes a Christmas party, complete with caroling. I had never been caroling as an adult, but after I went with the crowd from the saloon, the holidays took on a special meaning for me. About twenty of us loaded up in a horse trailer filled with straw that first frosty Christmas I spent in Montana, and someone said it was about ten below zero. We were all bundled up and made sure there were lots of blankets and hot chocolate for the kids and schnapps for the adults. The last one aboard was an enormous nanny goat named Blanche, and as we pulled away from the bar, no one had the heart to throw her out. The owner of the saloon had carefully printed out carols for us, so we practiced as we drove along the dark roads, lit only by a moon that peeked in and out of clouds.

When we arrived at the first house, we alighted from the trailer and sent someone to knock on the door. A light snow began to fall as we started in on a hearty "O Come, All Ye Faithful," and when the aged rancher who lived alone in the tiny log cabin was finally able to open the heavy door, I noticed how his eyes lit up and the pallor left his unshaven face as he watched the red-cheeked children with snowflakes melting on their lashes sing with everything they had. It was that way everywhere we went, and some people even had us all in for hot drinks. The joy of the season had never been more evident to me. Even Blanche was included in the choral group until she got a little rambunctious during the singing of "Santa Claus Is Coming to Town" and started to eat our music. The final straw came when she wet the straw in the trailer, and we had to circle back by the saloon to drop her off. The evening was rounded off with the children's party. Donations are made throughout the year at local establishments, then collected at Christmas to provide gifts, and "Santa" sees that every child receives one . . . Santa being our local mayor dressed in the traditional red suit. One of the ladies from the church got on the old honky-tonk piano and let it rip with some more Christmas songs, and we snacked on cookies and candies we had all brought to share.

During hunting season the saloon opens its doors for breakfast at five-thirty A.M. Fred proved to be a hero one of those mornings after the power went off during the night throughout the valley. We wanted to feed the kids before school so we called to see if the saloon, by chance, had any way of fixing breakfast. They said they could cook because they had a propane tank, but there was no water for coffee because they had an electric pump on their well. No flies on Fred . . . faster than you could say "Ty-D-Bowl," Schmook was to the rescue. He went into the tank, note I said *tank*, of all our toilets and collected four gallons of water. Fred, the kids, and I showed up with our buckets and thermos bottles, and the water was heated on the grill. Every hunter was able to have a cup of coffee before going out for the day. We didn't explain where we had gotten it, just chalked it up to local ingenuity.

Las Vegas has never appealed to me, and I would rather send Daniel Ortega money for a new leisure suit than throw it away in a slot machine or at a blackjack table in Nevada. But it's hard to resist slipping a quarter in a poker machine at the saloon. Certain types of gambling are legal in Montana if you are eighteen, and the saloon offers two of them. There are keno and draw poker, both in electronic game form. If you win, the machine prints a ticket, and the bartender cashes it for you. I have seen people win as much as one hundred dollars, but I have also seen people lose as much as three hundred dollars. That's a lot of quarters.

Kathy Schmook

I have seen only two fights occur at the saloon, and they were over the predictable. Some fishermen from Ohio walked in one evening while a group of us were sitting out front on the benches visiting and commenting on the spectacular sunset falling across the mountains. One of the fishermen, who had obviously never been west of his garage, made a grave error as he stood at the bar and picked up a cowboy's hat from his head, placed it on his own, and said, "Howdy, pardner." The fisherman came through the screen door and past us outside as if he'd been fired from a cannon. Actually, that was all the fight there was to it. The cowboy was already back to his beer, and the other fishermen were involved in a pool game. Old "Howdy" spent the rest of the evening sitting in his RV wondering why his nose had suddenly taken a left turn.

I am embarrassed to say that the other "encounter" involved my son, who was merely defending the honor of his dog, Ug. Some college-aged ornithologists from New England were on their way to Yellowstone to make a comparative study of the Western bluebird in relation to the Eastern one, and they had stopped off at the saloon. Fred and Bruce were also having something cold when Ug nosed his way through the front door, headed for the pool table, jumped up, found the eight-ball, took it and laid down by the jukebox. He did this all the time, so none of the locals batted an eye, but the only boy in the group of birdwatchers shrieked to one of the girls, "My God, Totie, would you look

172

at that ugly dog standing on the pool table . . . if he slobbers on me, I'll die!" He nearly did.

"He is disgusting," she replied. "I'm sure he must be rabid."

Now granted, "Ug" *is* short for "Ugly," and we named him that the day he appeared on our doorstep. He closely resembles a wild boar crossed with an alligator on long legs. His snout must be six inches wide, and it's flat with brown-and-white freckles on it. He has no neck and only one ear stands up; the other one has been shot so many times it lies down. The consoling thing about Ug is that most of the other dogs in the valley look like him since he is a prolific breeder. Rumor has it that he has on occasion endured the unpleasantries that only a skunk can offer for a mere "toss in the hay," so to speak.

But the bird boy had insulted Ug in front of his adoring owner and that was nearly the kiss of death.

"Who you calling ugly?" Bruce asked the boy, who was slurping on a diet Cherry 7-Up.

"I beg your pardon, sonny, are you talking to me?" he asked insipidly as he peered over his round horn-rimmed glasses.

"Yeah, I sure am, four-eyes, and you owe my dog an apology," Bruce said as he walked over to the table.

"Isn't this cute, it seems I have incurred the ire of the owner of that horrid-looking dog," he said as he turned to smirk at his table of friends.

Bruce brought a fist from nowhere and caught the boy right on the chin, which knocked him out of his chair and onto the hard wooden floor.

The boy stumbled to his feet holding his jaw and turned to Fred, who was sitting on a bar stool. "Is that your brat?"

Fred nodded, "Yep."

"Well, what are you going to do?" the boy asked as he adjusted his glasses, which were hanging off one ear.

Fred turned to Bruce and said, "Nice shot, kid, but you shoulda broke his glasses," and he and Bruce left with Ug on their heels.

We are fortunate to have The Old Saloon. It is not only a port in the storm, but it is an important landmark of the area. It's one of those establishments that transcends its owners, of which there have been many, because it retains its own ambiance . . . it is a mirror of the valley, composed from a composite of the personalities that frequent it. The names and faces of the patrons change, but the saloon doesn't. With its frozen water pipes in one or both johns four months out of the year, it continues to serve the warmest beer in the summer and the coldest beer in the winter.

Somehow I know that as long as an institution like The Old Saloon is around, I must be living in the right place.

There's a Church in the Valley

Being from the Bible Belt of the Deep South and proud of it, I might add, I was brought up to believe that a church forms the backbone of any society. If I thought it before, I'm convinced of it now, after living in a sparsely populated rural area for a couple of years. While it is quite obvious to me that Montana is topographical proof that God saved the best till last to create, it is paradoxical in a way because life is a struggle for the natives in a ranching community. Therefore, there is no room for a church that merely gives lip service to its members. It is imperative that the church fill many needs.

Then, too, I am attempting to raise two children who are not dummies and who question the ways of the world. They are aware of the Christian chicanery we are all subjected to, and they need to be taught that God does not work part-time for H & R Block; nor does He smile on the public figures that make a mockery of marriage and force their spouses to hide their heads in shame. Children are confused by a society that holds up highly paid athletes and entertainers as gods only to learn later they suffer from human frailties, too, ranging from drug addiction to strange sexual proclivities. And there are cults and new-wave religions abounding that offer solace and answers to the lonely and vulnerable, even promising a better life next go-round, provided you donate all your worldly possessions (which means flash the cash) to further "the cause" this time around . . . the cause being sure to keep the chief in high cotton at the expense of the Indians, who are not allowed to ask questions. Again, it is mandatory to the education of children for a church to act as an anchor, a constant in a world of variables. I found such a place.

I remember the first time I went to the tiny white clapboard church. I had never been in a church so small. It would have fit in the balcony of the large one I attended in the city. But it was beautiful inside, with its twelve oak pews and wainscoting and the delicate linens on the altar. There was an organ in the front and a piano in the back, and I have since learned that they have always been played by whoever showed up with the talent and/ or desire required. Only one lady knows how to play the organ, but we have several to choose from on the piano.

It wasn't until recently that there was a choir, and even it ranges in size from two (including the piano player) on up. They practice once a week, and if there are not enough people to sing at rehearsal, the choir director, alias local beautician, headquartered in the general store, goes next door to the saloon and strong arms some of the pool players into practicing with them. I have never made it through one of the choir's performances without shedding tears. When they did "The Old Rugged Cross" I cried, because some men sang and the harmony was magnificent; when they did "All Hail the Power Of Jesus' Name" I cried, trying not to laugh because we did not have a piano player and the only person present who volunteered to play had been taking lessons only a month and could play only the treble clef . . . which she did and got every other note wrong.

Our fearless leader is Father Michael, and, boy, does he have his work cut out for him. He oversees two churches, one in the town nearby and ours in the valley. I have never known a man who lived so totally by faith. It is an inspiration to watch. He once climbed the Tetons because he felt directed by the Lord to do so. He was led to take French lessons, which he did for over a year, and when he felt he was supposed to go to a school in France one summer, he went, not knowing why but resting in the assurance that it was God's will for him. He still doesn't know why, but his MasterCard bill is a constant reminder that he was obedient anyway. He does not pretend to be a deity and his appeal to me is his lack of fear in showing a very human side. He once asked our tiny congregation to pray for a wife for him. He would love to share his life with a woman because he does get lonely at times . . . a very human emotion. Much like the emotion Jesus showed in Gethsemane when he realized he was headed for the cross . . . alone. He does not type out a neat sermon every week, but instead waits until the service begins, then approaches the pulpit and preaches about what the Lord has told him needs to be discussed. Maybe it's God's unconditional love for His people correlated with love and fidelity in marriage; or maybe it's about loving one another and helping neighbors in need; or possibly the power of prayer in everyday life while one is milking, shearing or cutting hay. He never knows until he begins.

We pray different prayers in church, certainly not the kind I was used to. I did not understand the relevance at first, but after living here awhile, I do now. I was accustomed to praying for an end to racism, nuclear testing, for shelters for the street people and reduction in crime (I usually had to throw in something about hopes for a decrease in my condo rent), all major concerns for city dwellers. In my church now, we pray for good markets for sheep and cattle and a good hay or alfalfa crop with plenty of rain and snow in the spring to supply ranchers with moisture in the summers for adequate irrigation. I must admit I do throw in one for the wind to die down a bit on occasion, just so I can get my garden in without my seeds ending up in Wyoming. Then there are the prayers for controlling the forest fires that break out and destroy our timber and the grasshopper infestations so destructive to crops. We even pray for the safety of hunters during hunting season. There're also prayers for the unemployed, who may be not only suffering financially but also fighting depression and anxiety as well. That in turn can lead to alcohol abuse and breakup of the home, loneliness, despair . . . a vicious circle. Father Michael sees that we cover it all. We don't just pray for the sick in general either. If you're sick in our church, you get mentioned by name, including your ailment, unless of course you're sitting on it.

Because our church is so small, it is necessary to devise all sorts of ways to raise money to support it in addition to the tithing of the members. In the large churches I attended in the city, the stewardship drive lasted a whole month! It took that long to collect money from the massive congregation. Sometimes men on the stewardship committee even came to your house. How embarrassing! Now, Father Michael reminds us when it is time to make our pledges, and we all know that we need to contribute in order for our little church to sustain itself. There are no dramatics from the pulpit aimed to create guilt in members that may not be able to give right then. It is not necessary. The church continues to reach out in love and offer a "Give what you can, when you can" philosophy which tends to attract the truly cheerful giver, not the obligatory one.

We also sell pies at the social hall during elections, we hold pancake suppers, and we had a cake auction that raised $250 with only five cakes. Some of the children made the cakes, then walked them around during the bidding. One six-year-old had his Snickers cake slide off the plate onto the floor. He picked it back up and put it on the plate. It sold for seventy-five dollars.

Our baptisms are more dramatic than they were in the huge sanctuary where I attended church before. Back then, the sophisticated minister held the baby up like a flower arrangement for the church filled with thousands to admire. Then he made us raise our hands and promise to help raise the baby in the Christian faith, which I think meant you were supposed to call the head minister if you ever saw the kid in later years scribbling on walls or trying to OD on Milk of Magnesia. It's not like that in my church now. If you want to get baptized you go in the Yellowstone River, and I guess pray for a wet suit to drop from heaven on the way in. I saw one of the most moving baptisms I'll ever see last summer when a sixteen-year-old girl was completely submerged in the river during a light rain. A polar bear would have had trouble keeping his lips from turning blue. She stepped lightly from the river, and her mother wrapped a blanket around her. She had an enormous smile on her face, and I heard one of her friends say, "Gosh, I cannot, like, believe your parents made you do that . . . aren't you freezing?" To which the ethereal young lady replied quite succinctly, "They didn't make me. It was cool!"

Maybe that's it. Our church is cool. It picks up on the needs of its members and ministers to them. We have a small prayer group that meets during the week, led by Father Michael. We pray over the concerns of the church, the valley and each other. During that time, there is such devotion, trust, and faith in the little sanctuary that at times I think we're going to pray the roof off the place. At other times, I feel that God is so close to us, I want to say, "'Scuse me, shall I move over?" and offer Him a seat beside me. We also firmly adhere to the policy that a group that prays together can ski, ride, hike, and camp together, and we do. We have been known to adjourn from a particularly uplifting day of prayer and head to the saloon to celebrate answers to prayer.

There is a special Friendship Fund set up to help people through difficult times, and it is able to supply clothes, food, a temporary home, or maybe just money. It has helped send kids to camp and supported young adults in youth ministries. It is exciting to be a part of a church that does the work of the Lord without asking why. There is no judgment of anyone who doesn't attend on a regular basis, nor does it matter what you wear. Jeans and boots are the dress for most, and I must confess I have heard Father Michael ringing the bell and dropped what I was doing in the yard, rushed down the road only to enter my pew and realize I hadn't combed my hair and was still in my sweat clothes.

On the first Sunday of the month we take potluck to have lunch after the service. We have communion also, as we do every Sunday. That is always a treat because there is no telling how long the wine has been around, and sometimes it has a real kick to it. Unfortunately, on one particular Sunday, we had run out, and Sarah, Sunday school teacher par excellence and procurer of spirits, Holy and otherwise, dashed over to the Old Saloon to borrow a bottle. Half of our members left the altar with their cheeks sucked together . . . the MD-20/20 was a little much. Unbeknownst to me, my son's dog, Ug, had followed Bruce and his cohorts on foot to church that day. They had hidden him in the Sunday school room, but their teacher, Sarah, insisted he stay outside because none of the children was paying attention to the lesson. I suppose she wearied of arguing, and Ug was let in to watch the final minutes of the video showing of *The Lion, the Witch, and the Wardrobe.*

Kathy Schmook

When it was over, the children were let out to join their parents in the church service. Bruce swore it was an accident, but as he took his seat beside me and the offertory hymn began, Ug made his way slowly down the aisle, sniffing madly. He made his way up to the altar, and after a quiet rebuke from Father Michael, he rolled over on his back, spread his legs open wide and straight up, doing one of his better dead-bug imitations. He also smiled, which makes most people think he's going to bite because he curls his lip up on one side and shows his teeth, but in actuality he's the spitting image of Edward G. Robinson without a cigar. Bruce quietly got on all fours and crawled out into the aisle so Ug could see him and called softly. Luckily, Ug responded to his master, and Bruce was able to stand and lead him out. The stalwart piano player continued with another verse of "Onward, Christian Soldiers," using both hands now. That was the good part. The catastrophic part was that Bruce shut the sanctuary door but did not shut the door from the outside leading into the fellowship room where all the potluck food was. When we next saw Ug, he was standing on a table, just finishing up a yummy fruit-and-marshmallow confection. He had already devoured one plate of sliced ham, some German potato salad, macaroni salad, an apple pie, and a plate of brownies. He didn't touch my baked beans garnished with beanie-weenies. My sister, who was visiting, was duly impressed and asked if we allowed horses and cows in too. I told her only if they can play the piano.

So the diminutive church continues as it has for years in its undaunted and, at times, unrecognized effort to bring the nature of God out of the sky, out of the Bible, and into the valley. It is small but dignified, and it speaks with a whisper, not with the roar of an opulent church adorned with ornate spires or a cathedral of crystal panes. It makes no promises it doesn't keep, nor does it pretend to be something it is not. It seems to say to the passer-by, "Hey, take a load off, come and rest here for a while. I won't ask where you have been, but I'll sure help with where you're goin'." As my son said to Ug that fateful Sunday, "You can't act up in there, that's where God lives!" And so it is.

Happy Trails

I still don't ride very well, even though I have started rumors to the contrary, and I have yet to ski a black diamond at Big Sky. I dread the Colter race again this year, and Emigrant Peak seems to get taller still. But the challenges remain, and I look forward to new ones each day.

My son has decided to become a shepherd and spends his time tending his flock of three sheep and a goat while Lisa has given up watching MTV on our satellite to attend 4-H meetings.

I do not drive carpools, attend picayune meetings, or do any comparative shopping. In fact, I don't shop at all. I prefer to spend my time selfishly, either lounging around a trout pond with Fred or possibly mothering the countless critters that wander in and out of our ranch.

Kathy Schmook

I was interviewed years ago by a Junior League publication and asked what my life's ambition was. I replied flippantly that it was to have a happy family and a home filled with laughter. It seemed so easy back then. The road since has been circuitous, and it has involved taking risks, self-sacrifice, and a rearrangement of priorities, but, by golly, I think I'm finally getting it!

Glossary of Western Terms

SO THAT GENTLE readers can feel at home on the range and make their way through this book, I offer this brief glossary of Montana terms.

ANGLER—A fisherman or an attorney for an ex-spouse; both found to have the capability of telling a great story and expounding on the virtues of the one that got away.

BRAND—Cruel but efficient hieroglyph burned onto the hide of a cow, horse, mule or an occasional philandering cowboy by his wife.

BUCK FEVER—Malady which overtakes zealous hunters when they spot wild game. Causes a loss of reason and can make even Bambi appear to be a raging bull.

BUGLE—Noise made by a bull elk to let the other guys in the area know that he has staked out his territory and he is out to woo any gals around. Sounds like a mule who got his ear slammed in a door. Cannot dance to it.

CARRION—Not necessarily what they let you take on a plane; in fact, if it is found anywhere near a plane, the carrier is put in the baggage compartment. It is decaying meat and smells like chitlins do while they're cooking.

CATTLE GUARD—A series of iron bars sunk over a hole that makes a br-r-r-r sound when tires drive over it. It is used instead of a gate to keep livestock in an area. Horses spend most of their lives learning how to walk through or on top of them. Karl Wallenda is rumored to have a book coming out to teach horses and cows "the art of balance on the cattle guard"; it is entitled *Walkin' My Dogie Back Home.*

CRICK—A small stream of water that may have fish in it. Formerly referred to in the South as twitch in the back of the neck.

CREEK—A crick in Mexico.

COWBOY—One who tends cows. They are witty, friendly, and fearless. It has been said a cowboy will fight till Hell freezes over, then skate with you on the ice.

CHAPS (prairie pantaloons)—Leather pants worn over jeans by cowboys to protect the rider's legs from injury in case he is thrown into barbed wire or possibly bitten or kicked by his horse; also protects against wind or cold. Pronounced "shaps." Anyone heard pronouncing it "chaps" will be given a leather purse, banished from the West, and sent to Ralph Lauren as an apprentice in designing his new "It Smells So Good I Could Wear It" line.

DITCH—A hole on the side of the road that fills with snow in the winter and seems to have magnetic tendencies to attract cars. Also refers to water which may or may not be mixed with alcohol. Most important to watch for tadpoles in that case.

DOCK—Process which makes it impossible for lambs to wag their tails behind them because their tails are cut, clipped or banded. A punk sheep look.

EAGLE—Many of these reside in the mountains of the West. They are the symbol of the United States, sort of the President of birds and real snooty about it. Only hang out with other eagles.

FLY—Fake thing made of feathers, chenille, fuzz, glitter, fur, and other stuff found on the bottom of any pocketbook and wrapped around a hook. It is then fed to a deaf, dumb, and myopic fish.

GOPHER—Small animal similar to a chipmunk, good for absolutely nothing. They are capable of digging holes in a pasture ranging in size from just big enough for a horse's foot all the way to a family fallout shelter.

HACKLE—A long neck feather from a rooster used to make fishing flies from. Tricks fish into thinking it's finger lickin' good.

HEADING/HEELING—These techniques make up the sport of team roping. Two cowboys astride horses chase a steer, and one throws a rope for its head. If he is lucky enough to catch it around the horns or neck, he then jerks it bald-headed, and the other cowboy throws his rope at the two back feet. His hope is that by some miracle the steer will step into the noose he's thrown, then trip and fall down. At that point each cowboy has a tug-o-war over the steer . . . one pulling one way on the head, and the other pulling the other way on the feet. The steer is then untied and leaves looking like a meat stick. A truck driven by the Pakistani owner of a local convenience store usually waits in the wings and loads those steers up to take to the Slim Jim factory to be bottled.

KNAPWEED—A prolific weed that does have a pretty purple flower but is still considered the kudzu of the West.

LARIAT—A rope with a noose on the end used to trip a cow, catch a kid, hang a horse ("When I saw him, I thought of you")—trader and anyone mispronouncing the word "chaps" when not referring to blokes or lips.

OUTFIT—Not what is bought for Easter or the first Junior League meeting in the fall. It is a vehicle, usually a pickup truck.

OUTFITTER—Entrepreneur pathfinder who takes bored businessmen into the woods with guns, then ducks for cover as they shoot anything that moves, including squirrels, their horses, and, on occasion, the camp cook.

PEMMICAN—Contrary to popular belief, this is not a bird of Florida but a highly enriched meat, nut, and berry dried strip designed to sustain any trapper, Indian, hunter, or cowboy during grueling hours outdoors. No one who has ever eaten at Tour d'Argent or 'laillevent would touch it on a bet.

PROD—A long stick with a small electric charge in it that is used to fire up rodeo stock before they come out of the chute. It is also used by the mothers of teenage children in an attempt to get them to relinquish phone lines and clean the knapweed out of their closets.

ROCKY MOUNTAIN OYSTERS—That part of a bull's anatomy that is double-wrapped and hung in the shade. Should never actually be chewed because teeth have no traction on them.

SNORT—Sound made by startled and angered male (buck) deer or gaseous hunter after a hefty meal of pemmican.

SPURS—Metal anklets worn on the outside of boots that seem to encourage horses to perform their beast of burden duties with more enthusiasm. The CIA has reported in Kiev that Russian scientists are experimenting with cowboys and spurs in an attempt to launch the first child into space. Children are mounted on Andalusian stallions and told to kick them as hard as possible using some sharp spurs. The last kid tracked was somewhere between Uranus and Pluto.

STETSON (conk cover)—Very fine hat made for cowboys that is rolled and mashed around until it fits and suits the individual. Keeps sun and dust off the neck and face while wrangling also. It replaces the yuppie's visor and the baseball fan's cap.

"YOU BET"—Phrase used throughout Montana by virtually every resident. It takes the place of "Uh-huh," "No problem," "I know that's right," "Prego," and "I'll say." The only time it would never be used would be if a Montanan were asked if he were sorry that there weren't more folks living around him. The reply then would be "Are you crazy?"